Draw Floor Plans and Elevations With AutoCAD

2018

Version 2018

James Beebe

Building Designer, Drafter,
Building Contractor,
Construction Consultant

Structural Press

ISBN-13: 978-0-9848631-6-7

Preface

**Get a FREE TRIAL OF AUTOCAD Software
at AutoDesk.com**

This book teaches how to draw a Floor Plan and Elevation as you would need to get a permit and/or give to a builder for the purpose of constructing a project. It uses a project—**drawing a Floor Plan and Elevation**. This is an excellent way to learn because it teaches all of the processes and commands in AutoCAD and all of the necessary design elements. After completing this course you will be able to draft any floor and elevation for any project This is an enjoyable way to learn because it is project orientated and the drafting begins immediately. The drawing evolves quickly; this creates a feeling of rapid progress. This is quite different from other manuals that require many hours of learning in preparation for drafting.

This book is a carefully designed **programmed learning system** where every sentence has been crafted to fall into the proper order. The instructions build upon each other, step by step, to make the process flow naturally. Great attention has been paid to including every step of each process in plain English. Jargon has been avoided as much as possible. It is designed for people who wish to learn how to draft, not for the computer wizard.

Many of you will agree with the statement that help menus are often of little help. The same can be said of many software manuals. There are several reasons for this.

First, the language is often incomprehensible. The writers know how to use the software, but they don't know how to speak in plain English.

Second, steps are omitted from the instructions, often the first step(s). The writer assumes that the reader knows some of the steps.

Third, many manuals are presented in encyclopedic format. They list the various procedures, commands, and functions in sections without context. And they try to cover the entire program even though only a portion of the program is essential to most users. The essential information is buried in a sea of relatively unimportant information. **We don't need to know how to do everything in these programs; we just need to know enough to get the job done.**

Fourth, because we don't know the jargon, we can't ask for help. Without the words we can't formulate the questions.

This book addresses all of these problems. It goes straight for the **goal: how to draw Floor Plans and Elevations**. It does this by guiding the reader through the creation of a set of house plans with every step illustrated and described in plain language.

This makes for a dynamic learning experience because the drawing begins to take shape in the first pages and progresses at a rapid pace. The floor plan in Chapter 1 is completed in four to six hours.

Note: This book is an exerpt from AutoCAD in 20 hours. It includes chapters one, two and six from that book.

If you want to learn how to draw a full set of plans my book **AutoCAD in 20 Hours** will teach you everything you need to know as well as all the skills to be a compotent 2d AutoCAD drafter.

Visit the website at: **www.AutoCADin20Hours.com** for more information.

Important Note:
Read the Introduction before you begin. It contains information you will need to begin.

Table of Contents

Introduction

READ THIS BEFORE YOU BEGIN

Often we skip the introductions because they contain a lot of promotional material and not a lot of substance. **This introduction contains important information.** Take a few minutes and read through it.

This book covers all of the procedures and commands to draw any Floor Plan and Elevation. It uses Imperial measurements because that is (unfortunately) what is still used today in the United States for Architecture. This should not be an impediment for metric drafters. All of the measurements are called out in exact numbers and **no math is required**. The conversion to metric is not difficult and is explained. It is the **drawing skills** that are important and this is an excellent method to learn those skills as architectural drafting covers almost every situation that will be encountered by any drafter.

The house drawn in this book is designed to facilitate the learning process. It is not meant to be an award winning design. Some design components are less than optimal to speed up the drawing process. It is a very small house so that each view can be printed on 8.5 x 11 paper and on a typical small printer. But the home is fully functional and could be built. The completed plans would pass inspection in any building department, though additional drawings and notes could be requested. Some jurisdictions would require engineering.

AutoCAD is a huge system. It can perform very complicated operations. But most of us do not need all the complex features. This book teaches the essentials, based on the concept that the drafter can then draw anything in 2d. More complex methods and procedures can be learned later.

The huge size of the AutoCAD program causes **glitches**. There are hundreds of system variable settings that can change through some glitch. Sometimes the program locks up. Sometimes, when opened, the settings from prior sessions will be lost. Sections of the drawing can become locked up and "unselectable". The command line can disappear. It would take an entire book to catalog all of these possible glitches. This creates a problem for an instruction manual because it is not possible to predict when these glitches may occur.

Usually if things are not working, it is because the instructions are not being followed to the letter. But if there is a glitch, it can be difficult for the reader to evaluate.

If you are unable to obtain the demonstrated results, start by assuming that you have left out some part of the procedure. Read the text carefully and try again. Read the command line to see if the system is picking up on your input. If you still have a problem, see if there is an appendix listing for the command. Read Appendix I—Glitches. If you have access to the videos (see www.AutoCADin20hours.com), you can review the procedures there. If all else fails and you think that it might be a glitch, try restarting the program. If that fails you will have to research online for your problem. That should eventually produce the solution.

A very common glitch is that the system does not recognize the selection of a command when you click on a button. This seems to run in shifts—it happens for a while and then ceases to be a problem. When this happens **double click** the buttons. The problem should pass after a while and you can go back to a single click.

The system is setup for automatic saving. When the system **saves**, it **freezes** all actions. This can take a minute or more depending on the size of the file and the power of the computer. So, if you are drawing and the system freezes, wait a minute, it is probably saving your file.

Often, in the beginning, you will get stuck in the middle of some procedure and nothing seems to work; when this happens, use the escape button on your computer and start again. The escape button is a major tool in AutoCAD.

Often you will see a blue or green rectangle on the screen and nothing will respond, use the escape.
Read the command line as you go through the different procedures. The prompts tell you what to do and you can see if your input matches the prompts.

All of the drawing in this book is done in one file. In other words: **do not create a new file for each chapter**. Open the same file each time and do all your drawing in the same workspace.

Enter means to hit the enter button on your keyboard (see Appendix I—Keyboard). **<e>**, **ent** and **enter** are all the same: press the enter key.

In the Imperial system the quote symbol (**"**) means **inches**, the apostrophe symbol (**'**) means **feet** as in 10' 4" (ten feet four inches).

You can **type commands** instead of clicking on the buttons. But if you do this you will have to type the command and then **enter**. Clicking on a button **equals** typing the command **and** hitting the enter key. This can be confusing because some procedures require clicking a button and then hitting the enter key. For these procedures, if you type that command, you will need to enter twice. You'll figure it out now that you have read this.

Many of the parts of the drawing are created **off to the side in open drawing space**. This means anywhere on the screen. These are meant to be copied or moved later, so the original location of these parts of the drawing is not important. Similarly a lot of the instructions indicate an approximate location for certain objects or text. **Approximate** means put it anywhere close to where it is depicted in the figure.

Don't worry about making things really precise. That is not an important aspect of this learning process. The idea here is to learn the drafting methods and procedures; precision is something that you can work out later. So if you are uncertain exactly where to place something, or exact dimensions, let it go and just keep moving forward with the lesson. Of course precision is essential to drafting, but that is something you can work out on your own.

The **Osnap** or Object Snap feature places your objects in a precise location that is marked by an icon that appears when your cursor approaches certain predetermined points. You don't need to understand this now; you will understand when it happens. If an Osnap icon is highlighted, your object will **attach to that point**. Sometimes this is not what you want and you will want to turn off the Osnap feature to resolve this problem.

Sometimes AutoCAD **switches layers automatically** (you will understand this later, also). Watch for this in the Layer Control window displayed on the first page of Chapter 1.

Some readers will want to rely mostly on the illustrations and skip from one to the next. If you choose to use the book this way, you should still skim the **bold text** to make sure that you have not skipped over something essential.

Try to complete the entire book in as short a time frame as possible. This will insure that you retain the previously learned material as you move forward. If the study is stretched out over weeks or months it may require review or even starting over with the process. The best method would be to take a four day period and spend a few hours a day. If you can learn to draw floor plans and elevations in AutoCAD in four or five days, it will be an accomplishment. It takes most people months.

Note: This book is an extract from the book AutoCAD in 20 Hours.

Chapter 1—Setup and Floor Plans

Read the Introduction, before you begin, for some important general information.

1.1 Setup

Most books on CAD design begin with an extensive set up. This book takes a different approach. We will do the minimal amount of set up and start drawing. This will get things moving along and the set-up will be introduced as it is necessary to continue drawing. If you are unable to perform any of the tasks refer to Appendix I for trouble shooting.

When you first install AutoCAD you will see the screen in Fig 1-1. Yours will be black. This doesn't matter. I set my color scheme to white so it can be seen more clearly.

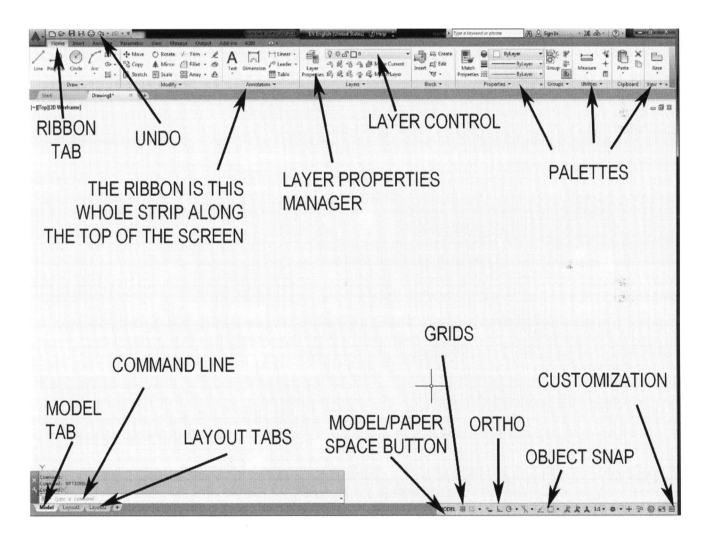

Fig. 1-1

If your screen displays boxes (not shown here) in the drawing area, close them by clicking on the x's.

If you see a different ribbon at the top of the screen, click on the Home tab. You may have more tabs than are shown here, don't worry about that for now. (If you want to add or eliminate tabs right click on a tab and select Show Tabs, then check or uncheck the tabs you want on the ribbon.)

The ribbon is the row of tools at the top of the screen as shown in Fig 1.1. There are a number of tabs along the top of the ribbon (Home, Insert, Annotate, etc.). If you click on these tabs you will see that a section of the ribbon opens that relates to the tab label. Within each section there are buttons associated with each command.

You do not need to know about these commands at this time as we will present them as they are needed to draw.

First we must set the measurement units to imperial standard for architectural drawing. AutoCAD will draw in metric or Imperial units. This book is written using the **imperial standard**—feet and inches. That is what is used for architectural drawing and construction work in the U.S.

Type **startup** (you will see the word appear in the Command line display, see Fig 1-1), hit **enter**. Type **1** then **enter**. This determines which menu you see when you open a new file.

Click on the AutoCAD icon in the upper left corner of your screen as shown in Fig 1-2. Select **New** at the top left corner of the screen. The pop up box shown in Fig 1-3 will appear (you may get a different box first, if so, click on the **quick set up** option to get this box).

Fig. 1-2

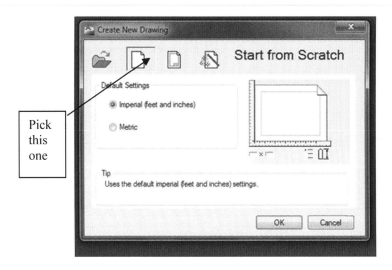

Fig 1-3

Click on the button shown in **Fig 1-3**.

Select the **Imperial (feet and inches)** button as shown.

Click **OK**.

If you need to know where to find a particular button use the F1 button, or type help. In the help homepage window that opens select **Commands**. There you will find an alphabetical list. Select the first letter of your command and scroll down until you find the command you are searching, click on that command and a box will open that shows the location of the button explains the process for its use.

Fig 1-4

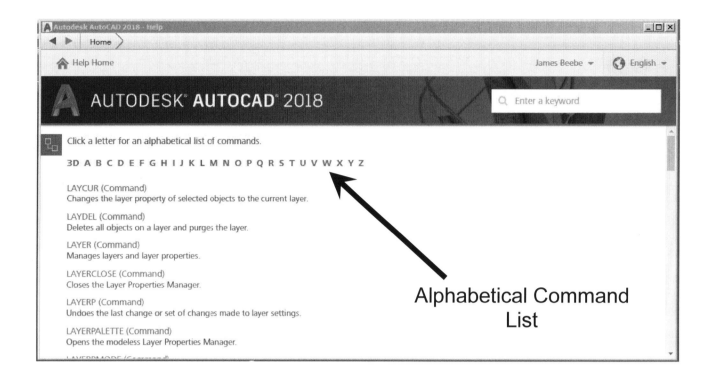

Fig 1-5

All the commands can be typed instead of clicking on the buttons (type the word for the command: **Line**, **Trim**, **Erase**, etc). However, if you type a command the procedures may be different than as described in this book. Most commonly you will need to press the enter key on your keyboard after you type the command. The **buttons equal: typed command + enter**. In this case the "enter" key sets the command in motion. Otherwise the typed command just sits in the command line waiting for some action.

If you lose the command line hold down the control button on your keyboard and press 9 on your keyboard. If this does not work type commandline and enter.

Down at the bottom of the screen you will see a row of buttons. If you **position** your **cursor** arrow **over** any of **them** and **do not click** (this is called: **hovering**) they will **tell you their names** (Fig 1-1). **Turn them** all **off**, **except** the **Ortho** and the **Object Snap** (we want these two turned on).

You can turn **Object Snap** on and off by pressing the **F3** key on your keyboard. The **Ortho** command can be turned on and off with the **F8** key. Object Snap is also called **Osnap**.

Now right click the **Object Snap** button. A selection box will open. Click on: **Open Object Snap Settings**.

A dialog box will open called **Drafting Settings** as shown in Fig 1-5A. Take a moment and look at the tabs at the top of this box. Here are the settings for the commands that are controlled by the buttons at the bottom of your screen as shown in Fig 1-1.

Select the **Object Snap** tab at the top. Turn on the following: **Endpoint, Midpoint, Intersection, and Perpendicular** (as shown by the leader arrows in **Fig 1-5A**). Turn off all other object snaps.

Click on the **OK** at the bottom to close the menu box.

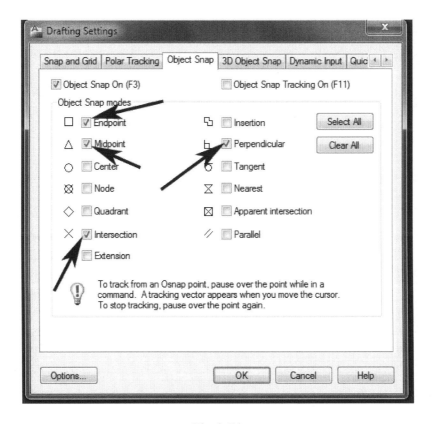

Fig 1-5A

Turn off the grids by clicking on the **Grid display** button in **Fig 1-1**.

1.2 Line

We are ready to draw the floor plans. Before we begin take a quick look at the completed floor plan so you know what we are doing. You will find them at the rear of this book in Appendix IV. Look at the last figure in this chapter (Fig 1-63) to see the drawing we are going to draw in this chapter.

Before we begin an **important notice**: the apostrophe symbol (') represents feet in the Imperial system. The quote symbol (") represents inches. As an example 12 foot is 12' and 6 inches is 6". 12 foot 6 inches is 12'6". **You must type the foot symbol after a number that represents feet** or you will get the default (which is inches). It is not necessary to type the inches symbol (") because **inches is the default** (though it won't hurt to use this symbol).

Let us take a moment and turn off the **UCS**. This is the X and Y coordinates graphic in the lower left of the screen.

On the ribbon click on the View tab. All the way to the left you will see the UCS Icon button. Click on it. The USC will disappear from the screen.

Often AutoCAD does not set the units that you select in the start-up. Check to make sure they are set correctly by typing the word: **units**. When the Drawing Units window opens set the **Type** to **Architectural** and set the **Units to scale inserted content** to **inches**.

On the **Draw** palette click on the **Line** button (click the Home tab to see the Draw palette).

If strange things start to happen, or you get into trouble, hit the **Escape** on your keyboard, or click on the Undo button (Fig 1-1), and try again.

After you click the **Line** button, move your cursor over into the drawing area. It will turn into a cross. (If it doesn't look like a cross see Appendix I—Cursor.) Click anywhere in the drawing area and move the cursor down. You will see a line. (This line should be locked into the vertical—straight up and down—if it is not, you must turn on the Ortho as detailed above). Now type: **27'** and press the **enter** key. Press **enter** a second time.

Type: **zoom** (all you need to do is type the first letter **z**—many commands only require the first letter of the word) and Enter (press the enter key on the keyboard).

At the **Command line** (Fig 1-1) at the bottom of the screen you will see a list of options. Type: **a** and **enter**. (As you type, look at the command line and read the prompts: **a** = all.)

Use your mouse wheel to zoom out a bit (see Appendix I—Mouse Wheel). You will see the vertical line you drew. It is 27 feet long. Sometimes this doesn't work when you first start a drawing and the line disappears when you enter. If you have a problem, see First Line in Appendix I.

Click on the **Line** button again. Position your cursor (the cross) at the upper end of the line and an object snap box will appear (Object Snap must be turned on). Click on this box. Move your cursor to the right a short distance. You will see a horizontal line. Type: **22'** then **enter**. Do not enter a second time as you did before.

You will see a 22' line. Move your cursor down and pull out a line. (If this doesn't work click on the Line button again). Type: **27'** and **enter**.

Now position the cursor near the bottom of this line and draw towards the left. When you get near the end of the original first line you should see a snap object icon. Click on this icon and hit **enter**. You should see Fig 1-6.

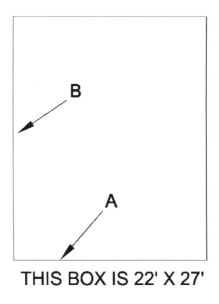

THIS BOX IS 22' X 27'

Fig 1-6

You do not need to click the Line button each time as long as the next line starts at the end point of the line you just drew. Just position the cursor near the end of the last line and pull out a new line in the direction that you want to draw. Watch the prompts that appear in the command line to see where you are in the sequence.

1.3 Offset

Click on the **Offset** button in the **Modify** section of the Home ribbon:

Type **5'** then **enter**. (Look down at the Command line when you type and read the prompts.) The cursor will turn into a box. Place that box over the lower horizontal line A in Fig 1-6. The line will illuminate; click on it. The cursor will turn back into a cross. Move the cursor up above line A a bit and click (anywhere above is fine). A new line will appear. It is 5 ft from the lower line. Press the escape key on the upper right corner of your keyboard.

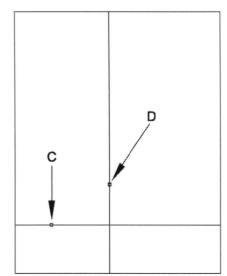

Fig 1-7

Click on the **Offset** button again. Type **10'** and **enter**. The cursor will turn into a box again. Position the box over the vertical line B in Fig 1-6. The line will illuminate. Click on that line. Move the cursor to the right a bit and click. A new vertical line will appear. Press the Escape key on your keyboard again. You will see the drawing on the left in Fig 1-7.

1.4 Trim

Click the **Trim** button on the Modify palette (it is co-located with Extend, see Appendix II for help). Press **enter** (**from here on <e> will mean to hit the enter key**). The cursor will turn into a box again. Position the box on the center vertical line somewhere near the middle as in D in Fig 1-7. It will illuminate. Click on it. It will erase the upper part of the line, leaving the lower five foot section.

Press the Escape key on your keyboard. The cursor will return to a cross. (Note: you must press the **enter** key on your keyboard immediately after you click the **Trim** button for it to function in this manner. If you do not hit enter right after you click on the Trim button it works in a different way—see Appendix I-Trim for an explanation.)

Click on **Trim** then <e> again and this time click on the point indicated by **C** in **Fig 1-7**.

Click on the **Line** button again. Position the cursor (cross) over the upper right corner (E in Fig 1-8) of the rectangle and click. Move the cursor to the right a little and type: **12' <e>**. A new horizontal line will appear.

Move the cursor down from the far right of that new line a bit and type: **22' <e>**. From the bottom of this line move the cursor to the left and when it gets near point F in Fig 1-8 click on the osnap icon that appears. Press the **Escape** key again. You will have a drawing that looks like Fig 1-8.

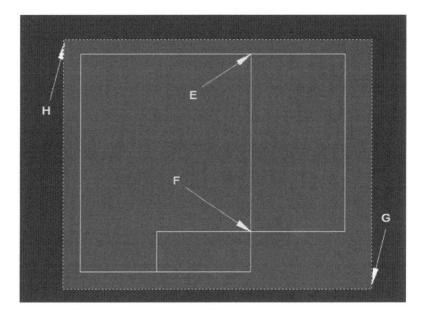

Fig 1-8

Zoom out by using the wheel on your mouse. (Sometimes AutoCAD locks up and won't scroll out. If this happens type: **zoom <e>** then: **a <e>**. Now the wheel should work.) Zoom out until the drawing is about a quarter as tall as the drawing area (see Fig 1-9).

Click on the **Copy** button On the Modify palette. The cursor will become a square (box). Position this cursor box to the right of the drawing a bit and down below the drawing a bit as shown by **G** in Fig 1-8. Press the left button on the mouse, release the mouse button (the cursor box will disappear) move the mouse up and to the left. A **green** window will form. Enlarge the green box until it covers the entire drawing and **click at approximately H** in Fig 1-8. Completely cover the drawing with the green box before you click the left mouse button again. The lines covered by the green selection window will be highlighted and the little cursor box will reappear. This indicates that all the lines that were inside the green selection window have been selected. Press **<e>** (enter). Read the prompts.

Now position the cursor somewhere in the center of the drawing you just selected and click. **Move** the cursor to the left of the drawing a distance more or less as you see in Fig 1-9 and click then **<e>**. Use the mouse wheel as needed to zoom out. This will make two separate views of the drawing. Press the **Escape** key. You will have two drawings and they will look (more or less) like Fig 1-9.

1.5 Selection windows

When you cover items with the green shadow box, like we just did, you must include all the parts of the drawing to be selected within the green shading. See Appendix I—Selection Window for an explanation of this. (There are other ways of selecting elements to be copied that we will discuss later.) If you end up with only part of the drawing copied then you will need to erase or undo the flawed copy and try again. Use the Undo button at the top of the screen (or Ctrl Z which is the typed command for Undo).

This second copy of our drawing will be used later to create other views of the plans (ie: Foundation).

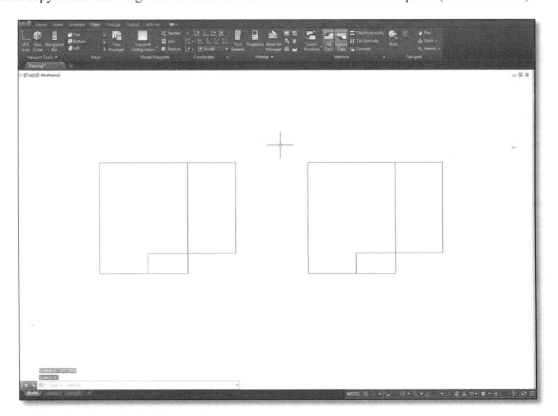

Fig 1-9

You can move around in the drawings by holding down the mouse wheel and **Panning** (Appendix I—Panning). Try this. Escape from all commands, place the cursor in the drawing area, hold down the mouse wheel and move the mouse around. If you don't have a mouse with a wheel, buy one. It makes life so much easier in AutoCAD land. If you can't afford one then use the zoom features to move around (described a little later). Let us return to our original drawing. Zoom in on the drawing to the right. Use the mouse wheel (place the cursor in the center of the drawing then turn the mouse wheel) to scroll in and enlarge it until it fills the page (see Appendix I—Zoom if you do not have a mouse wheel). Hold the mouse wheel down and pan the drawing until it is centered in the drawing space.

Let's add a new line. Click the **Offset** button. Type **6'6 <e>**. Position the cursor on the top horizontal line (**I** in Fig 1-10) and click. Move the cursor down below the line a bit and click. A new line will appear. Press the **Escape** (from now on to be abbreviated to **Esc**) button on the keyboard.

Add another line (for the stairwell—see the final floor plan if you need a reference). Click the **offset** button. Type **5' <e>**. Center the cursor box on the middle vertical line (J in Fig 1-10). It will illuminate. Click. Move the cursor to the left a bit and click. A new line will appear. Press **Esc** on the keyboard. Now the screen should look like Fig 1-10 (your drawing will not show the little boxes).

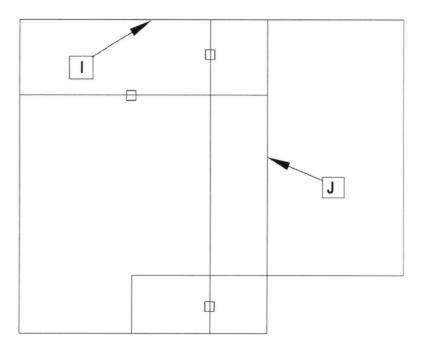

Fig 1-10

Now we will trim some more lines.

Click on **Trim** then immediately **<e>**. Position the cursor over one of the lines indicated by the **little boxes** as shown in Fig 1-10, click (do not enter after clicking on each of these points—just go on and click all the trim points). Click on all the points indicated by the boxes in Fig 1-10. Press the **Esc** button on the keyboard. You should now see Fig 1-11.

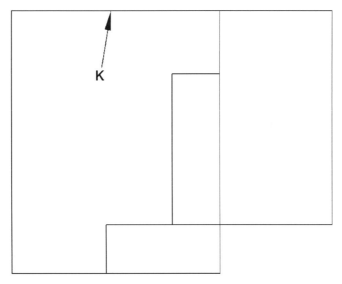

Fig 1-11

1.7 Walls

Figure 1-11 shows the outline of the first story floor plan. Now we will draw the wall thickness. Click the **Offset** button. **Type 3.5 <e>**. AutoCAD uses inches as the default. So if you enter feet you must designate this by using the feet sign: ('). For inches no sign is necessary. This measurement is inches.

Position the cursor on the top horizontal line (K) and click. Move the cursor down below this line and click. A new line will appear 3.5 inches below the top horizontal line. This is the thickness of that wall (nominally a 4" wall—but drawn at 3.5" because they are framed with 3.5" wide lumber).

Now let's repeat this process with all of the walls. Click Offset, position the box cursor over the far left line and click. It becomes highlighted. Move the cursor to the right of that line (any distance will do) and click. Repeat this process by drawing parallel lines on the sides of the single lines as shown in Fig 1-12. You will see that it is not necessary to hit the Offset button each time. The tool remains active until you press <e> or ESC. We are creating the thickness of the framed walls. Continue until you see Fig 1-12.

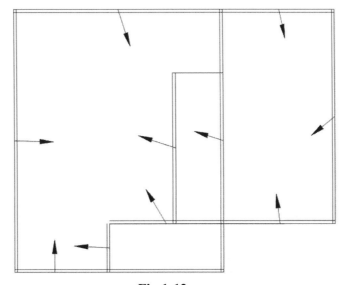

Fig 1-12

As always, do not get too caught up in the perfection of the details, if you miss something, or draw it incorrectly, you can fix it later. The main thing is to keep moving along and learn the commands and procedures. Precision and accuracy will come with practice.

Next we are going to clean up the inside corners of the walls. Click on **Trim <e>**.

Sometimes the buttons don't respond; if this happens double click them. Also you can always type any command.

Use the mouse wheel to zoom in on the upper left corner of this plan drawing. **Click** on the point indicated (approx.) by **L** in **Fig 1-13**.

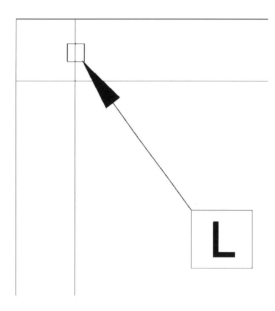

Fig 1-13

This will trim the line to the lower intersection of the lines as in Fig 1-16.

Use the **Trim** tool, position the cursor box over the lines in the rest of the corners, and trim the lines so that they all look like **Fig 1-16**. Remember to hit the enter key <e> **immediately after clicking** on the **trim button**.

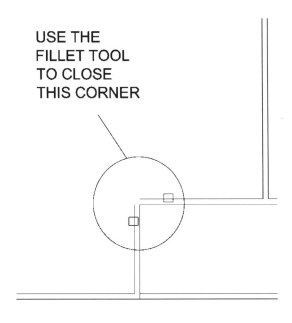

USE THE
FILLET TOOL
TO CLOSE
THIS CORNER

Fig 1-14

1.8 Fillet

To close up the open corner in Fig 1-14 use the **Fillet** tool on the modify palette.

Click the **Fillet** button on the Home ribbon. At the command line it will prompt you for options. Read the Command Line. Type: **r <e>**. This selects the radius setting.

With many of these prompts typing the first letter of the word is sufficient to choose that option. The command line will ask you to specify radius. Type **0** (zero) **<e>**.

Now it will prompt you to: **select the first object or**... Type **m** (for multiple) **<e>**. The cursor will change to a selection box again. Click on each of the two lines at the boxes shown in Fig 1-14. The corner will close (square). **ESC**.

Let's make a copy of this working drawing, as we did before. Click the **Copy** button. Enclose the main drawing that you have been working on with a **green selection** window and make a copy to the right so that the screen looks like Fig 1-15. To do this click **copy**, then click the cursor to the **lower right** of the floor plan, then **draw** the **green shading** up and to the left until the entire floor plan is covered, **click again** to select the floor plan. Next **click** the cursor in the middle of the floor plan and then **click** again in the **open space to the right**. This is an approximate location (the exact location is not important). We will use this new copy for the second story floor plan and the framing plans.

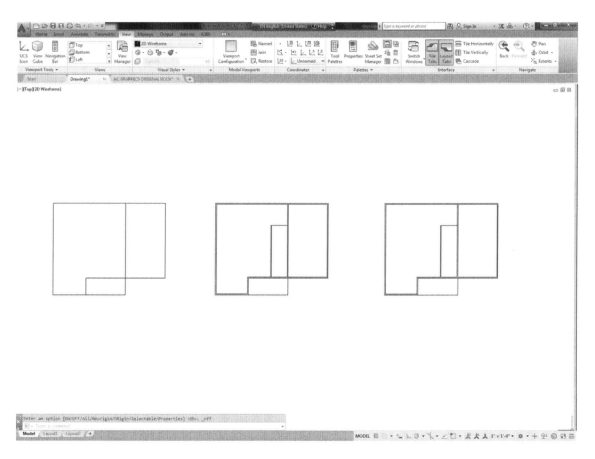

Fig 1-15

Sometimes the zoom will lock up and not zoom out enough. If this happens use the **Zoom** command –type **z<e>** then type **a <e>**. Now the mouse wheel should work.

1.9 Zoom

Take a minute and play around with the zoom options. Try some of the buttons on the **Navigate** panel. Click on the **View** tab. Right click anywhere on the panel and select **Show Panels**. Select the Navigate option. The navigate panel will appear on the ribbon. Click on the arrow in the lower right corner. Click on the **Extents** button. The entire drawing should appear.

Now click on the **Window** button in that same menu. Then click the mouse at the lower corner of one of your three drawings. Use the mouse to create a selection box around a part of the drawing by clicking on the screen and moving the cursor up diagonally and click. You can always use the ESC button and the Undo button at the top of the screen to go back if you get in trouble.

It is faster to type these commands. Type z for zoom and then the first letter of the type of zoom (as in w for window).

The Zoom Window is useful, especially when used with Zoom All. But ninety percent of the time I use the mouse wheel for zooming. See the info in Appendix I—Zoom for more on the subject of Zooming.

Your working drawing should now look like Fig 1-16 (minus the text—the text is for temporary reference).

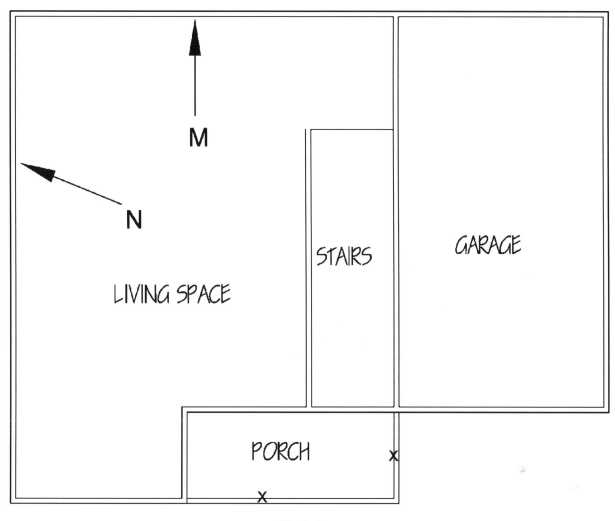

Fig 1-16

Erase the **lines** marked with **X's** in **Fig 1-16**. Click on them and then click the right button on the mouse. Select **Erase** from the menu that appears.

You can erase in a number of different ways. You can use the **delete** key on your computer keyboard, or click the **Erase** button in the Modify panel or enter erase at the command line. You can also select an item then right click and select the erase option.

You can select multiple objects and erase them in a group.

1.10 Kitchen

Click on the **Offset** button (Home tab/Modify palette). Type **24 <e>** (this will indicate inches—the default). Click on the inside line of the wall at the top of the living space shown as **M** in **Fig 1-16**. Move the cursor down and **click inside** the living space. Repeat the process with the wall to the left of the living space (N in Fig 1-16). **Esc**.

Click on the Offset button again and type **8'8 <e>**. Click on the new horizontal line (O in Fig 1-17) and click below that line to create new line (P).

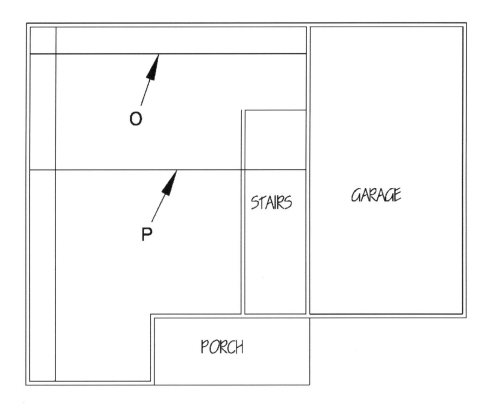

Fig 1-17

Click on **Trim <e>**. Trim the lines so that they look like **Fig 1-18**. If you make a mistake, use the Undo button and try again.

Escape.

Click on the line marked with an **X** in Fig 1-18 and **erase** it.

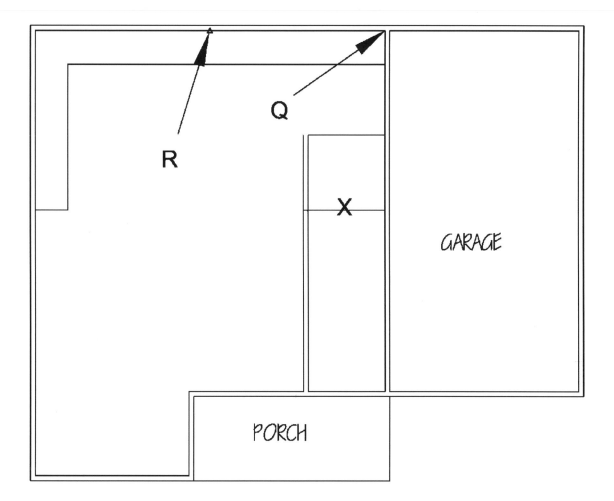

Fig 1-18

1.11 Offset Start Point of Line

Click on the **Line** button. Hold **down the Shift key on your keyboard and right click the mouse**. Click on the **From** selection. Now **click** on the inside corner point as marked **Q** in **Fig 1-18**. **Move** the cursor (now a cross) to the left along the horizontal line to point **R** and you will see a triangle icon (this is a snap object icon indicating the **midpoint** of this line). Do **not click on point R,** just let go of the mouse and let the cursor hover over the triangular Osnap icon. Type **7'5 <e>**. **Move** the **cursor down** the screen and **a line will appear** with a starting point at 7'5" from point Q. Pull the line down a ways, **do not click**. Type **3' <e>**. Hit **ESC**.

Sometimes when you make lines using the From function they do not attach correctly to the intended starting point. Zoom in and see if the line is attached to the horizontal wall. If it is not attached then undo and try again or see the Appendix I—Snap From.

Click on the **Offset** button. Type **3.5 <e>**. Click on the line that we just drew and click to the left of it to create a new short wall. At the bottom connect the ends to create the wall end as in **Fig 1-19** (use the Line button).

Trim the lines at the **X**'s in **Fig 1-19** (**you must press enter right after you click the trim button or it will not work as a trimming tool**). Escape and **erase** the line marked with an **O**. It will now look like Fig 1-20.

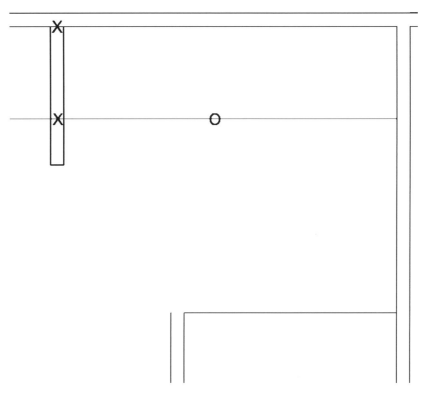

Fig 1-19

The new lines inside the living space at 24" offset represent the lower kitchen cabinets. Look at the finished floor plan in Appendix IV (or Fig 1-63) to see what we are drawing.

1.12 Rectangle

Now we will create the sink and the range.

Click on the **Rectangle** button on the **Draw** palette. It is in the upper right corner and shares a button with Polygon.

Click on the empty space somewhere in the middle of the living space (see Fig 1-20). Look at the command line. It prompts for a response (Area/Dimensions/Rotation). Do not move the mouse—your typing will automatically be entered into the Command line window. **Type d <e>. Type 30 <e>. Type 24 <e>. Click** (this last click sets the rectangle in place). **Make a copy** of the **rectangle**—so we have two as in Fig 1-20. Read the prompts as you follow these instructions. The **d** selects the **Dimensions** option (this is the most common method to create a rectangle). Then the numbers you enter are the dimensions (with the horizontal dimensions first, then the vertical).

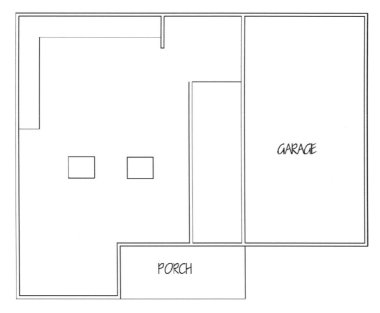

Fig 1-20

1.13 Rotate

Click on the **Rotate** button on the **Modify** palette. **Click on any line** of the rectangle on the left to select it and <e>. Read the prompts. The command line will read: **Specify base point. Click** (anywhere) **inside** the selected rectangle. **Type 90 <e>.** The box will now be at a 90 degree angle to its original orientation.

1.14 Move

Click on the **Move** button on the **Modify** palette. **Click on any line** of the box you just rotated, then <e>. **Click** on the **mid point object snap icon** as shown in step 1 of **Fig 1-21**. Move the rectangle around a bit. You will see that it will only move at right angles. We want to release the box to move free from this right angle constraint, so we will turn off the **Ortho**. Press the **F8** key. This will turn off the **Ortho** function (and the Ortho button at the bottom of your screen will un-highlight or pop out).

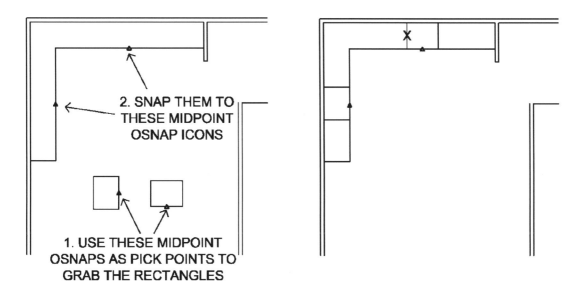

Fig 1-21

Move the rectangle and **snap it** to the kitchen counter at the center of the vertical section of the kitchen counter (the triangle to the right shown as step 2 in Fig 1-21) snap to the object snap **triangle icon** at the midpoint of the line shown. When you approach the midpoint of a line (with the midpoint osnap turned on) a small green triangle will appear. Click on this and the rectangle will copy to this point. It will **"snap to"** this point.

Now click on the **Move** button again and **select** the other **rectangle** (not rotated). **Grab** it by the middle of the lower line by clicking on the **triangle** icon (midpoint icon as shown in step 1). **Move** it up and place it on the center of the horizontal cabinet line at the midpoint icon for that line. Your kitchen cabinets will look like the right half of Figure 1-21 (minus the triangles).

Click on **Offset**. Type **3 <e>**. Click on the left vertical line marked X in the right drawing of Fig 1-21. Click in the center of the rectangle. **Esc**. This will create a parallel set of lines inside the rectangle as in Fig 1-22.

Click on the **Fillet** button on the **Modify** palette. Type **r <e>**. Type **2 <e>**. Then **m <e>**. Read the Command Line as you type, you will see that you are choosing the **first letter** of the various options offered. Click on the corners of the inside rectangle that you just created as shown in Fig 1-22 to create a radius corner at each corner.

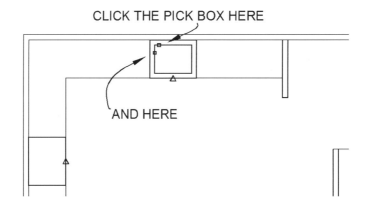

CLICK THE PICK BOX HERE

AND HERE

Fig 1-22

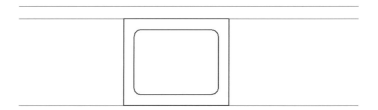

Fig 1-23

Click on the other corners of the rectangle; continue until the rectangle looks like Fig 1-23. This is the sink.

Now let's make the other rectangle into a stove. Let's find the center of the rectangle by drawing two lines that start and end at the midpoints as in Fig 1-24.

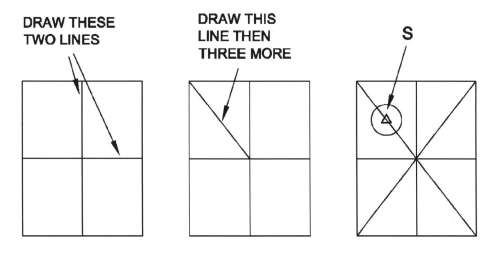

DRAW THESE TWO LINES

DRAW THIS LINE THEN THREE MORE

S

Fig 1-24

Now draw **four separate diagonal lines** as shown to the right in Fig. 1-22. (***They must be four separate lines to make this work, so don't cheat by drawing this with just two lines***). We will use these diagonal lines to find the center of each quarter of the rectangle by snapping to the center of each diagonal line.

Click on the **Circle** button on the **Draw** palette. Click on the **midpoint osnap icon** at **S** in **Fig 1-24**. Type **d <e>**. Type **6 <e>**. **ESC**.

Click on the **Copy** button and then **click** on the **edge** of your new **circle** and **<e>**. Grab the circle at the **center** by clicking on the **triangle** icon. Now copy the **circle** to the **center** of the other **three diagonal lines**. **ESC**.

Now **erase** the **diagonal lines** and the lines that cross the center of the rectangle. Your drawing will look like Fig 1-25.

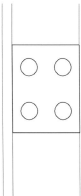

Fig. 1-25

1.15 Chimney

Now we are going to create the chimney and fireplace. Click on **Offset**. Type **8' <e>**. (Don't forget the ' symbol—you will get inches by default—you want feet.) **Click** on the lowest horizontal line at **T** in **Fig 1-26**. Move the mouse **up** and **click**. Right click the mouse and select **Enter** from the short cut menu box. This is a quick way of doing Enter. If no short cut box appears or one that doesn't include an **Enter** option then you can just press **<e>** on your keyboard (and see Appendix I—Mouse settings).

Click **Offset**. Type **12' <e>**. Click on the lowest horizontal line (**T** in **Fig 1-26**) again and then click again **up above** it and **<e>**.

Click **Offset** again. Type **18 <e>**. Click on the vertical line to the left (**U** in **Fig 1-26**) and then to the **left** of that line and **<e>**.

There is another way to do repeated tasks, like three offsets in a row. Instead of the final enter in the above steps right click the mouse and a shortcut menu will give you some options, the top option will be **Repeat** the last command, click on it. You can also use this to access a list of other commands. Check it out.

Using this flyout menu can speed up your drawing.

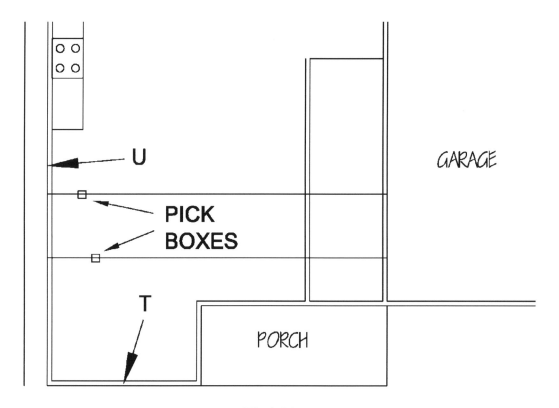

Fig 1-26

Your drawing should now look like Fig 1-26 (minus the references, pick boxes, and leaders).

1.16 Extend

Click on the **Extend** (co-located with trim) button on the **Modify** palette then **<e>** (you can right click the mouse to **enter**—with this function—if your mouse is set up this way. See Appendix I—Mouse settings). Click on the **lines** shown in **Fig 1-26** by the pick boxes. **ESC**. The lines should extend over to meet the new vertical line at 18" beyond the wall line as in Fig 1-27.

Extend is one of the more persnickety of the commands and sometimes it does not work the first time. If it doesn't work try clicking closer to the end of the line and, if that doesn't work, try again by escaping and re-clicking the Extend button then immediately press the enter key. See Appendix I—Extend for help.

Now your drawing should look like Fig 1-27.

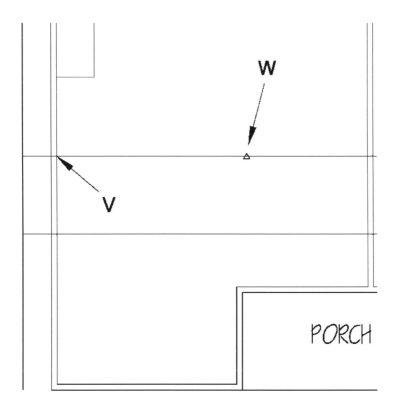

Fig 1-27

Click on **Line**. Hold down the Shift key on your keyboard and right click the mouse to bring up the Osnap menu. Select **From**. Now **click** on the intersection at **V** in **Fig 1-27. Move** the **cursor** to the **right along line W** in **Fig 1-27** until you **hover (don't click)** over the **midpoint** Osnap icon (triangle). Type **8.5 <e>**.

Turn the **Ortho on** (F8). Move the **cursor down** and to the **left** until a **vertical line appears**. You should have a stretchy line that **starts** at 8.5 inches to the right of point V. Pull the line down until you intersect with the line below. A **perpendicular osnap icon** should appear. **Click** on it. Then **ESC**. Now it will look like **Fig 1-28** (minus the text and boxes).

Sometimes the line created with the From command doesn't attach to the perpendicular line at the starting point. Then when you try to trim (as you will in the next step) it doesn't trim. If this happens erase the new line and try again or use the Extend command to attach it.

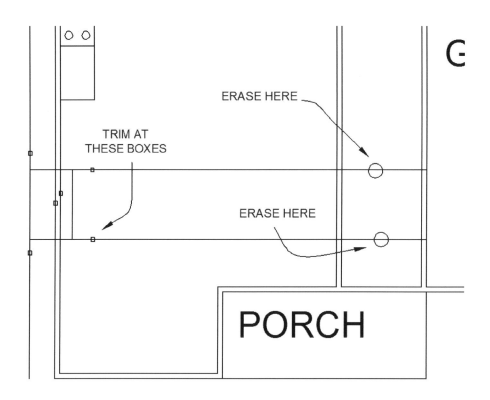

Fig 1-28

Click on **Trim <e>** and trim the **lines** at all the little boxes as shown in **Fig 1-28**. After you trim, **erase** what is left of the lines as shown in **Fig 1-28**. You will see Fig 1-29.

Fig 1-29

Click **Offset**. Type **5 <e>**. Click on the **top horizontal line** of this rectangle. Click below that line and **<e>**.

Right click and a menu will appear. Click on **Repeat Offset** (or use the old method and just click Offset). Type **14 <e>**. Click on the **top horizontal line** of the rectangle again. Click below. **Esc**. You will now see the two offset lines shown in Fig 1-30 (minus the diagonal line).

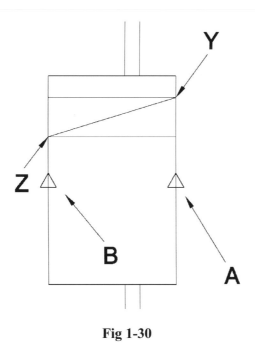

Fig 1-30

Turn the **Ortho off**. Draw a **line** from **Y** to **Z** in **Fig 1-30**. **Esc**.

Click on the **Mirror** button on the **Modify** palette. The Command Line reads: **Select Objects**. Click on the new diagonal **line YZ**. Then **<e>**. The Command Line reads: **Specify first point of mirror line**. Click on the middle of the right side of the rectangle on the **midpoint icon** that will appear when your cursor approaches the point shown as **A** in **Fig 1-30**. Move the cursor to the left and **click** on the middle of the other side of the rectangle (**point B**). Then **<e>**. You will see Fig 1-31.

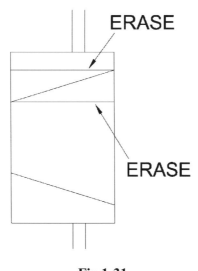

Fig 1-31

Erase the **lines** as shown in **Fig 1-31**. Click **Offset**. Type **3.5 <e>**. **Click** on the **sides** of this **rectangle** and create walls inside the rectangle to look like **Fig 1-32** (minus the boxes).

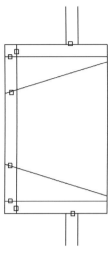

Fig 1-32

Trim the lines at the points marked with the **boxes** shown in **Fig 1-32**. The fireplace will now look like it does in Fig 1-34.

1.17 Door Openings

Now we will create the door openings. Click **Line** then hold down the shift key and right click the mouse. **Select From in the menu that opens. Click** on the upper left corner as marked **C** in **Fig 1-33**. Move the cursor down that same line to where it shows an **endpoint** icon at the chimney (point **D**). Hover over this icon, **do not click**. Type **11'6 <e>**. Turn the **Ortho on**. Draw a line to the right and connect to the **perpendicular** point icon on the other side of the wall at **E** in **Fig 1-33**. **Esc.** Zoom in. Click **Offset.** Type **32 <e>**. Click on the line you just drew and **click below** to draw the line at **F** in **Fig 1-33**.

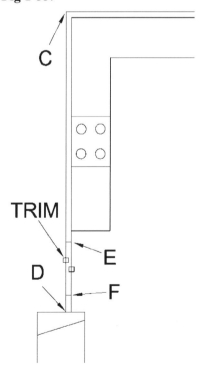

Fig 1-33

Trim the lines at the boxes shown in **Fig 1-33**. This is a door opening. Now we will **repeat** the process to create the door openings as shown here in **Fig 1-34**.

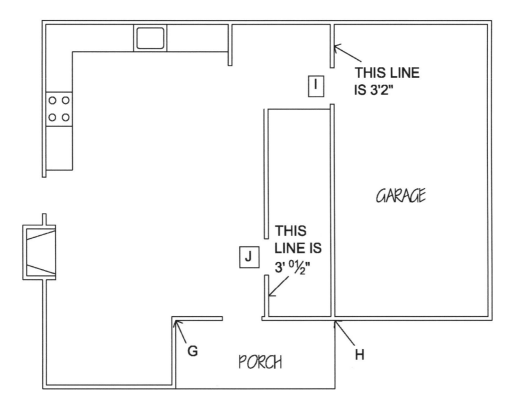

Fig 1-34

To create the lower door opening use **Line** then **From** (Shift + right click) and click on point **G** in **Fig 1-34** then **hover** over the osnap icon that appears when you approximate point **H** (do not click here—just hover). Type **6'6 <e>**. Attach the line to the other side of the wall as shown. Use the **Offset** tool to draw the other side of the door opening at **36 inches** offset, then trim the opening. This is the front door to the house.

Use the **Line** and the **From** buttons for the first line of all the openings. Use the **measurements** shown in **Fig 1-34** to draw the first line of each door opening. The dimensions shown are the offset for the first point of the door opening lines. They indicate the length of the lines shown after you trim for the opening.

The dimension that reads 3'-0 ½" is typed 3'0.5 <enter> (also 36.5 or 3' 01/2 works). Draw the first line, then use the Offset button to create the line at the other side of each door opening. The **door opening** sizes are all **32"** except the lower **(front) door** which is **36"**. Use the **trim** to remove the **lines** inside the door openings.

Now let's add the doors. Turn the **Ortho off**. Click **Line**. Click at point **K** in **Fig 1-35**. **Type: @32<315 <e>. ESC.** This is a new way to draw a line. The **32** is the **length** of the line and **315** is the **angle**. This is the easiest way to draw lines that are a specific length and at a specific (non right) angle. (See Appendix I—Polar Coordinates for an explanation).

Let's create the door swing arc. Click on **Circle** on the **Draw** palette. **Click** on **K** then **L** in **Fig 1-35**. You will see Fig 1-35. Make sure you click on the intersections and not the midpoints.

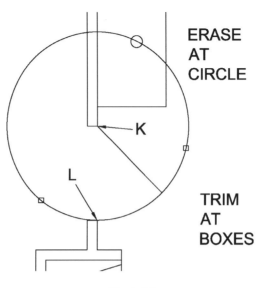

Fig 1-35

Trim the circle at the **boxes** and **erase** the remaining line at the **circle**. Now repeat this process for the other doors.

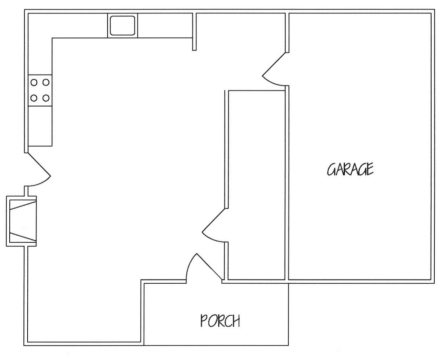

Fig 1-36

Remember the front door is 36". The measurements and angles that you need are: **@32<225** then **<e>** at the upper garage door **I** in **Fig 1-34**, **@32<225** then **<e>** for door **J** in **Fig 1-34**, and **@36<135** then **<e>** for the **front door**. Create the **arcs** for each door following the steps as before. You will see Fig 1-36.

When you input measurements you can always enter them as inches (you don't need to use feet). So the Offset from measurements that we used here for the first line of the bath door opening could be **36.5** or **3'0 ½ or 3'0.5**. **Remember inches** do **not need to be identified** because inches is the **default unit** of measure—no entry for units means inches.

1.18 Windows

Now we will draw the windows. First we will create a new layer. **Layers** in AutoCAD (as in a number of different graphic programs) are essentially a series of transparencies overlaying each other. They can be turned on and off for a variety of purposes, some of which we will explore as we go along.

To create a new layer find the **Layer Properties** button (see **Fig 1-37**). **Click it**. It may take a moment to respond. A **dialog** box will open that looks like **Fig 1-37**. You can expand this window by grabbing the side border when a double arrow line appears, hold down the left mouse button and pull. Also the border at the bottom down.

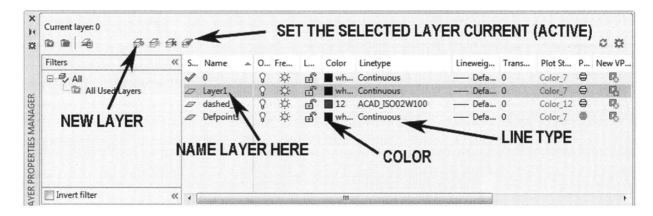

Fig 1-37

Click on the **New Layer** button as shown in **Fig 1-37**. A new line will appear. In the **Layer Name** window type: **windows <e>** to give it a name. Click on the **Line Color** where it says **white** or **w....** A **Select Color** box will open. Click on the **Index Color** tab at the top and select a **red box**. Click the **Okay** button at the bottom. Close the Layer Properties Manager by clicking on the x in the upper left corner.

Back in the AutoCAD main screen click on the **Layer Control** window as shown in **Fig 1-38**.

Fig 1-38

A drop down box will appear. **Click** on the **Window** line. Now the layers box will show the **Windows layer**. It will be set as the **current layer** (to use the correct jargon).

Fig 1-39 contains all of the information that you need to draw the windows. In each case, start with the center line as indicated. They are all located on the **midpoint** of a line; except the window over the sink, it is located on the **midpoint** of the **sink rectangle** upper line. Locate the **midpoint osnap** icons at the points indicated. Start the line at the midpoint icon then attach the other end of the line to the opposite side of the wall (at the **perpendicular osnap** icon).

Use the **Offset** to draw the lines **parallel** to the **center line** to create the ends of the windows (over the sink that will be 24 inches each way from the center, the **5'0"** window will be **2.5'** each way from center, the **2'6"** window will be **1'3"** each side of center, the **6'0"** window will be **3'** each side of center). Then use the **Line** tool and snap to **midpoint** again to create the line running the length of each window.

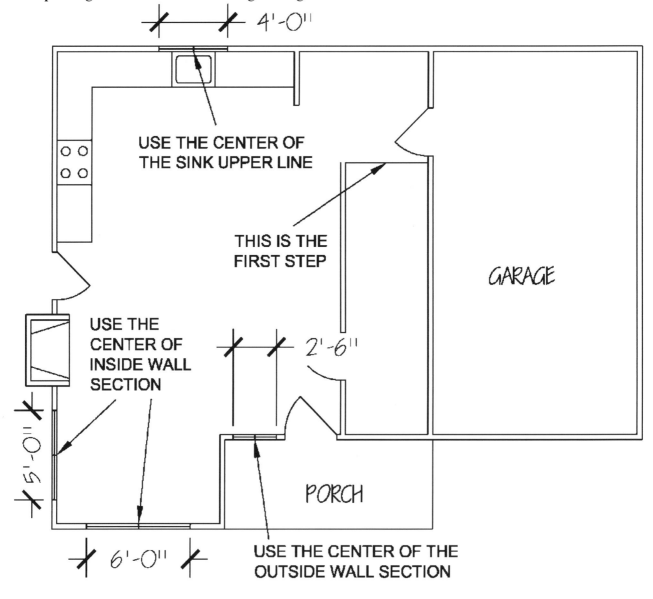

Fig 1-39

Now let's create the stairs. Click **Offset**. Type **10 <e>**. Click on the **FIRST STEP** line shown in **Fig 1-39**. Then type **m <e>** at the prompt. **Click** below that line and then below the new line and **repeat** until you have **11 lines**. This set of stairs will have 14 steps but we will only show 11 lines (including the first line) on this first story floor plan view because a portion of the bathroom is located below the stairs).

1.19 Design Center

We will now draw the bathroom fixtures. Start by creating a **new layer**. Go to the **Layer Properties Manager** again. **Create a new layer**. Name it **Fixtures**. Click on the Colors Designation and set it to white. **Close** the dialog box. In the **Layer Control** drop down box click the little arrow and select the **Fixtures** line. This will make the Fixtures layer the **current layer**. It will say: Fixtures in the Layer Control window.

Now on the **Palettes** palette on the View ribbon there is a button titled **Design Center;** it looks like this: . Click on it and the **Design Center dialog box** will open. You can also type: adcenter.

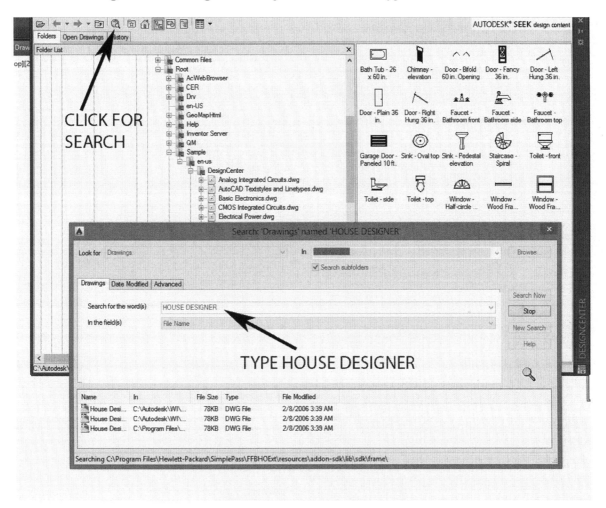

Fig 1-40

Click on the **Search** button as indicated in **Fig 1-40**. In the search window type: **house designer**. And Select the first search result below.

When the House Designer folder opens double click on the Blocks icon as in Fig 1-41.

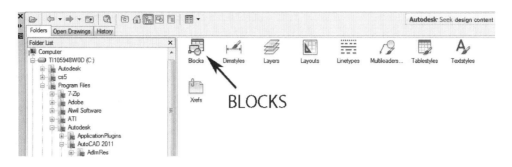

Fig 1-41

Center the **cursor** over the **toilet symbol**, hold the left mouse button down, pull it over and release the button on the AutoCAD drawing screen (not too close to the house) as shown in **Fig 1-42**. (This is called **drop and drag**.)

Do the same with the **Sink** symbol and the **Bathtub** symbols as indicated in **Fig 42**. **Close** the Design center box (click the x at the upper left corner).

An alternate method is to highlight the symbol (ex: toilet) right click, select the **Insert Block**, click on **Okay** in the **Insert dialog box** that pops up, then place the cursor on the drawing screen and click.

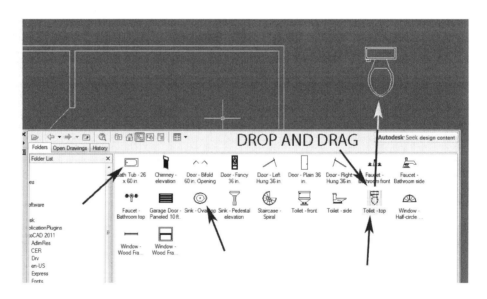

Fig 1-42

Now we will place the toilet and sink. Rotate the toilet. Click on the **Rotate** button on the Modify palette. **Click** on the **toilet** <e>. (Sometimes when you click on an object it will show little blue boxes and triangles, *you do not want this*, so escape and try again until the toilet appears as a highlighted line drawing as in Fig 1-44.) The prompt will read: **Specify base point**. This is the point you will rotate around. **Anywhere on the toilet** symbol is fine. **Click** and the prompt will read: **Specify rotation angle**. **Type 180** <e>. Now rotate the sink—enter **90** <e> for the angle of rotation for the sink.

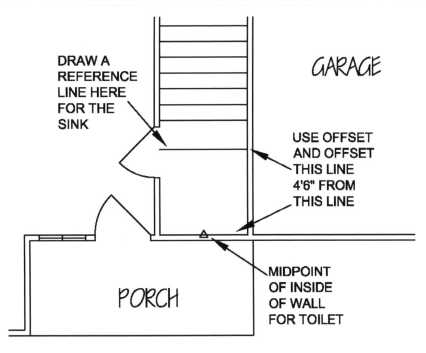

DRAW A
REFERENCE
LINE HERE
FOR THE
SINK

GARAGE

USE OFFSET
AND OFFSET
THIS LINE
4'6" FROM
THIS LINE

PORCH

MIDPOINT
OF INSIDE
OF WALL
FOR TOILET

Fig 1-43

Move the toilet. Click on the **Move** button on the Modify palette. **Click** on the **toilet** <e>. The command line will prompt for: **Specify base point**. This is where you will grab the toilet. Grab it at the **midpoint** of the back of the toilet as in **Fig 1-44**. Make certain that the **Ortho** is turned **off**. Drag the toilet and place it as shown in **Fig 1-45**. This is the midpoint of the inside wall section indicated in Fig 1-43.

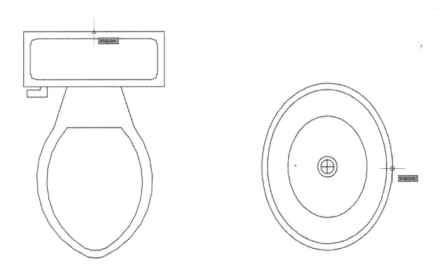

Fig 1-44

Create the **line** shown in **Fig 1-43** as a reference point for placing the sink. It is **offset 4'6"** (use the **Offset tool**) from the inside of the bathroom wall (see Fig 1-43). This a temporary line to mark a point on the bathroom wall—the point on the wall where we will snap the copy of the sink.

Now **move** the **sink**. Place the sink as shown in **Fig 1-45**. Snap the sink to the intersection of the wall and the reference line that you created. When you go to grab the sink you may notice that the icon you want is a box (endpoint as shown in Fig 1-44) and not a triangle (midpoint). This is because the sink is made up of series of arcs and lines. Erase the reference line when you have placed the sink.

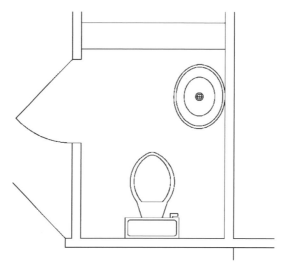

Fig 1-45

You can move the toilet and sink away from the walls with the Move button. Click **Move** then **select** the **toilet** <e>. Turn the **Ortho on**. **Click** on the **toilet again** anywhere. **Move** the toilet **away from the wall** a bit and **type 1** <e>. It will move it 1 inch away from the wall. Repeat for the sink.

1.20 Washer and Dryer

Now draw the washer, dryer and water heater and then our graphics will be nearly complete for the first floor.

Set the **0 Layer current**.

Create a square anywhere in open space that is **30"** x **30"**. Click on the **Rectangle** button then **click** in open space. Follow the prompts at the command line (**d** <e> for dimensions at the prompt, then **type** the dimensions **30** <e> and **30** <e>, then **click** on the screen to set the rectangle. If you have forgotten how to do this, review section 1.12.

Now **copy** the **square** to the places shown in **Fig 1-46** by **snapping** the **corner** of the box to the **inside corners** of the **walls**. Turn the **Ortho off** and the **Object Snap on** (F3). You will need to do two different copies: one for the right hand corner and another for the left hand corners. Click the **Copy** tool, then on the rectangle, then grab it by the corner osnap icon, snap this to the inside corner icon where you wish to copy.

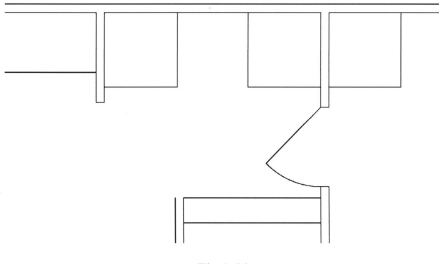

Fig 1-46

Now move the boxes representing the washer and dryer away from the walls one inch by using the **Move** button as we did with the toilet. Turn **Ortho on**. At the prompt for: **Specify base point**, show which way you want to move the rectangle by clicking on the rectangle, holding down the mouse button, moving it a bit in the direction you want it to move, and type **1** <e>. Repeat in the other direction until it looks like Fig 1-47.

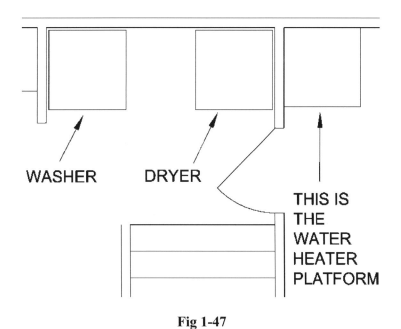

Fig 1-47

Now place the water heater on the platform (see Fig 1-49). Find the center of the square in the garage by drawing a **diagonal line**; draw a **24** inch diameter **circle centered** on the **midpoint** of the **diagonal line**. This is the same procedure that we used for the stove in Fig 1-24. **Follow the prompts**. If you are not finding the right osnap points, turn them on in the Object snap settings (see Appendix I—Object Snap).

Erase the diagonal **line**.

1.21 Text

We are ready to enter our text into the drawing. First **create** a **new layer** in the **Layer Properties Manager** and call it **Text**. Leave it white for now. **Set** this **Text** layer as the **current** layer.

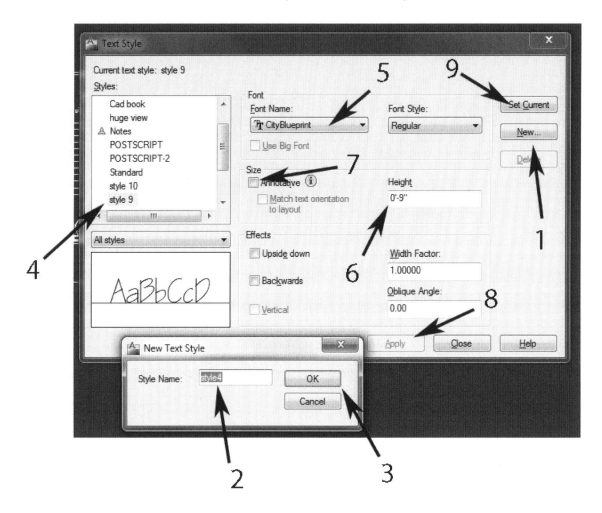

Fig 1-48

Now we must **create a text style**. Type: **style**. The **Text Style dialog box** will pop up (**Fig 1-48**). Click **New** (1 in Fig 1-48). **Name** the **style** in the window (at 2 in Fig 1-48), type: **style 9**. Then click **Okay** (3).

Back in the **Text style dialog** box **click the style 9 selection** (4). **Click** on the drop down menu under **Font Name** (5) and **select City Blueprint**. **Highlight** the **Text Height** (at 6 in Fig 1-48) and **over type**: **9**. **Uncheck the Annotative** box (7). Click **Apply** (8), then **Set Current** (9), then **Close** (see Appendix I—Text for more info).

Type mtexttoolbar in the command line and enter a value of 1. This will turn on the text formatting tool bar.

We will begin with the room/space designations. Type **mt <e>** (mt stands for Multi-line text).

Click on the **space** in the **middle** of the **kitchen** and move the mouse up and to the right to **create** the (approximate) **text box** that is shown in **Fig 1-49**. **Click** for the second corner. The exact size and placement are not important.

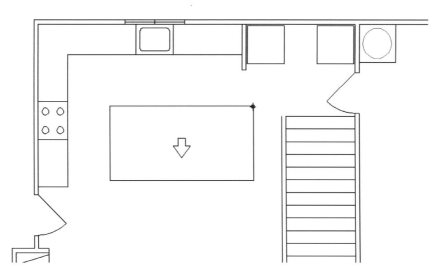

Fig 1-49

The **Text formatting bar** shown in **Fig 1-50** will appear.

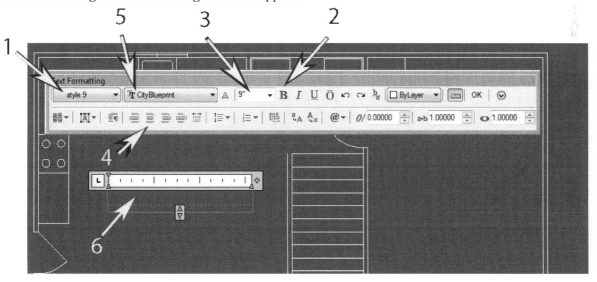

Fig 1-50

Set the **Caps Lock** on the computer keyboard (see Appendix I—Keyboard). **Select** your **style 9** (at **1** in **Fig 1-50**). **Click** on the **Bold** (2) button at the top of the bar. **Check** the **size** box (3) to make sure it reads **9**. If there is another number in this box then click on the number in the box, when it turns blue, **overtype** it with a **9**. Click on the **Center Text** (4). Check that the Font reads **City Blueprint** (5). If it is something different then you can change it in this window, but it is better to close this box, go back to Text Styles dialog box, and set it there.

Now type **KITCHEN** in the text box (6) on the screen. Click **OK**.

Click on the **Copy** button and then **click on** the word **Kitchen** <e>. The text (KITCHEN) must highlight before you can select it (if you have trouble selecting it then hover over it and move the mouse; you will see it change to a highlighted lettering—this means it can be selected). Now copy the word to the (approximate) locations shown in **Fig 1-51**. (Turn the **Ortho off** and **Object Snap off**). **Esc** when you have copied them all.

If your text doesn't highlight, then see Appendix I—Selection Problems. Your system settings might be wrong.

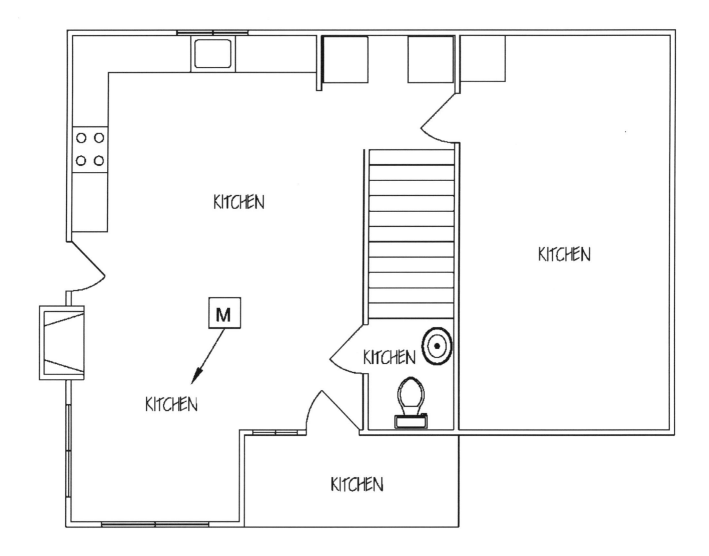

Fig 1-51

Now **click on** the lower left **KITCHEN** text at **M** in **Fig 1-51**. **Right click** and a drop down box will appear, choose **Mtext Edit**. The **Text Formatting** window will open as in **Fig 1-52**. **Highlight** the text (**KITCHEN**) by placing the cursor in the text box at **O** in **Fig 1-52** and press down on the left mouse button, hold it down, and scroll to the left. It will create a **blue selection window over the text**. Leave it blue and **overtype it with: LIVING ROOM**. Click **OK**.

Fig 1-52

Repeat the **text edit process** with the rest of the text until the drawing looks like **Fig 1-53**. Click on each of the Kitchen texts, open the Text formatting box, highlight the text and over write it with the text shown in Fig 1-53.

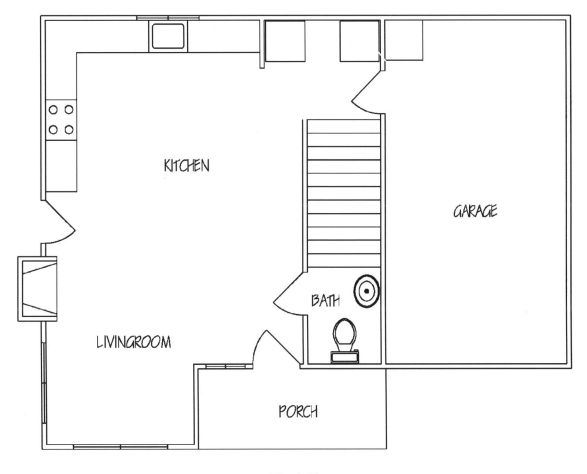

Fig 1-53

There are a lot of different ways to do each thing in AutoCAD. You can experiment with the different ways to approach the Text. I find this to be the easiest way to create multiple labels with the same properties. The standard way would be to open a new text dialog box for each piece of text. It is fine if you prefer that method.

Now we will create the window information text. Type **mt <e>**. Open another text box above the kitchen window at **Q** in **Fig 1-54. Highlight the 9"** in the text size box by clicking on it (it turns blue) and overwrite it with: **6** (see

Fig 1-50). Turn on the **Bold** button. Click in the text box (where the cursor is blinking) and type: **4-0 x 3-6 SLD**. Then OK.

> If the text doesn't appear in a single straight line then adjust the length of the box using the grip at **P** in **Fig 1-52** at the right side of the **ruler**. Place the cursor on the little arrows (or diamond) and hold down the left hand button on the mouse to grip the box and stretch it out to the right until the text appears on one line.

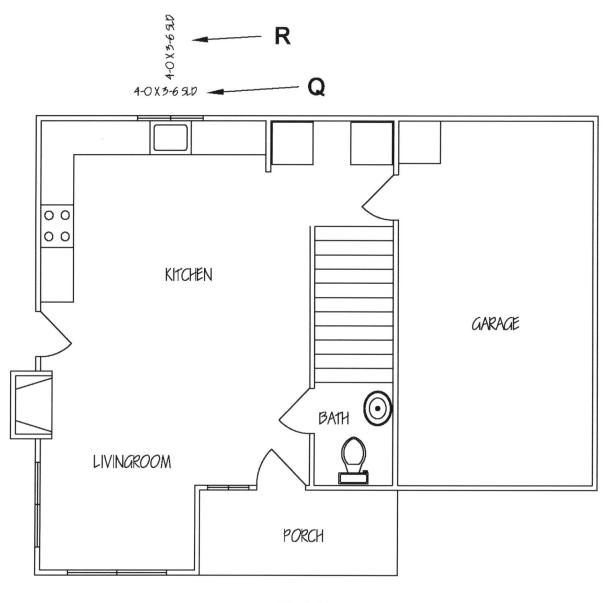

Fig 1-54

We are going to copy and rotate this text. **Copy** this text to the empty space above it as at **R** in **Fig 1-54** (this Fig shows it after rotation). **Esc**. The exact location of the copy is not important.

Click the **Rotate** button and then **click** on the **text** that you just copied <e> (at **R** in **Fig 1-54**). **Click** again on this same **text**. (Read the prompt: **Specify rotation angle or...**) type **90** <e>. This will rotate the copy to 90 degrees as it appears in Fig 1-54. Now **copy** these two versions of the text to the places shown in **Fig 1-55** (**Object snaps off**). Place the **text** by **hand** (no snap points—just place it by eye), roughly centered on the windows. Don't worry about placing it exactly for now—you can do that on your own drawings later if you choose. I place most of my text by eye—just as long as it looks good it is fine. Setting text to precise points is covered later.

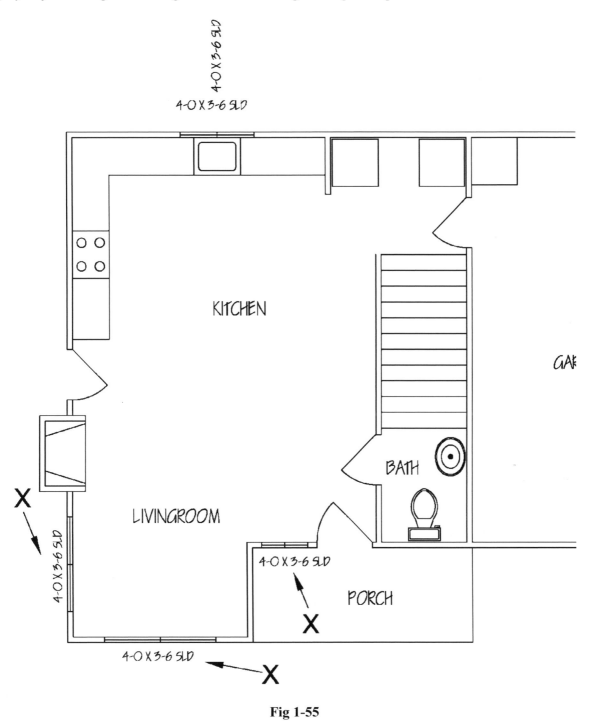

Fig 1-55

Click on each of the window size **texts** and edit them (highlight the text and overwrite it) to read as in **Fig 1-56**.

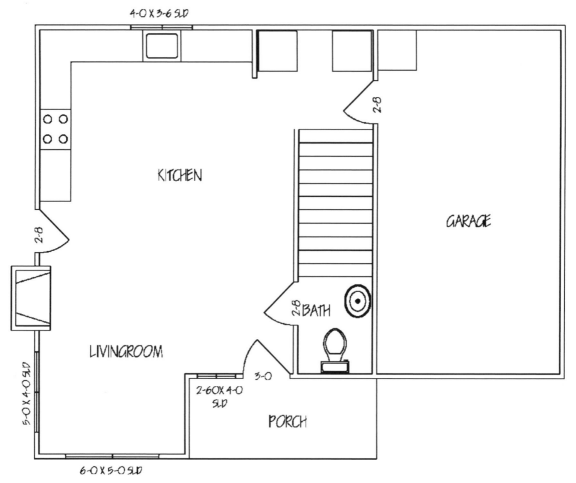

Fig 1-56

Use the **ruler** at the top of the **Text box** (**P** in **Fig 1-52**) to change the window label text on the porch to two lines as shown (you can also use the enter key between the numbers and the letters SLD to move them to a new line, as you would with any typing program). Check to make sure the **Text Centered** button is on (4 in Fig 1-50). If the text is not where you want it, click on the Move button on the Modify palette then use it to position the text where you want it (Ortho and Object Snap off). This doesn't always respond as it should, if you have troubles try stretching the text into one line, press the Center Text button, then shorten the box again.

Now **repeat** the process with the **door sizes** (use **6"** letter size and **Bold**); and with the washer (**W**), dryer (**D**) and water heater (**HW**) as shown in **Fig 1-57**. Use the **9"** text for these and **Bold**.

Now **add** a **note** for the **fireplace** as shown in **Fig 1-57**. Open a **mt** box and enter the information from the drawing below. Use **6"** letters and **Bold**. Use the Move command to position the text.

1.22 Odds and Ends

Okay we have just a few more items to add and the floor plans will be complete. Let's wrap up a few odds and ends. Turn on the **0 Layer**. Turn the **Ortho on** and the **Object Snap on**.

Close off the end of the wall at the stairwell with a short line (**Fig 1-57**).

Now open up the front of the garage with a **nine foot opening** as shown in **Fig 1-57**. Use the **exterior wall midpoint** as the center of the opening. This **opening is 9'**, so it will be 4.5' offset each way from the center line. Enter the garage **door size text** as shown below (use **6"** font and **bold**). You will need to have the Midpoint and Perpendicular Osnaps turned on.

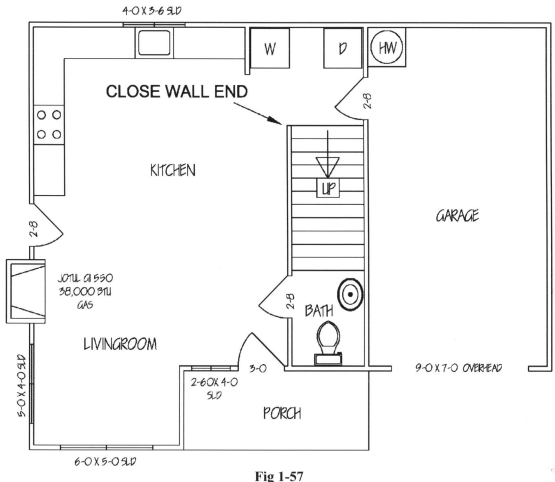

Fig 1-57

Make an UP arrow for the stairs (**Fig 1-57**). Out in open space (anywhere on the screen) draw a vertical **line 36"** with the **Ortho on** (see **Fig 1-58**). Now turn the **Ortho off.**

Click on the **Line** button and snap the start point of a new line to the bottom of the 36" vertical line as in **S** in **Fig 1-58**. **Type @18<60 <e>. Draw** another **line** from the top of this angled line back to the vertical line **T** and attach it at the **perpendicular** osnap point (left side drawing in Fig 1-58).

Use the mirror tool to create the other side with the mirror line being the 36" vertical line (T in fig 1-58). Click on the **Mirror** tool then **read the prompts**. When it says to **select an object**: select the **angled line** and the **horizontal line** and **<e>**. When it says: **select first point of mirror line**, snap to the **top** of line T. When it prompts for the **second point** click on the **bottom** of **line T** and **<e>**. Don't forget to enter.

Move this arrow and place it on the **midpoint** of the fifth step line using the **tip of the arrow** as the base point as in Fig 1-57.

Now in open space again, open a **mt** box (**type mt <e>**) and **type: UP**. Use **9"** and **Bold**.

Use the **Rectangle** tool and **create** a **box around the UP text** like the one in **Fig 1-57**. **Move** the **box** (just the box for now *not* the **UP text**) and place it on the end of the arrow (use the Osnap at the top midpoint on the rectangle). Now use the **Trim** tool (Trim + rt click or <e>) to erase the line inside the box. Now **move** the **UP** text and place it in the **center** of the **box**. Do this by eye for now, we will discuss precision text placement later. **Erase** the **box** and **trim** the **arrow** to appear as shown in **Fig 1-63**.

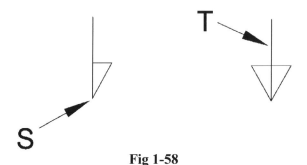

Fig 1-58

1.23 Dimensions

Now we are ready to enter the dimensions. We are going to use the non-annotative method. (Annotative text is covered in AutoCAD in 20 Hours,Chapter 16.)

To begin, create a **new layer** in the **Layer Properties Manager**. Name it **Dimension**. Leave it **white** (you can always change the colors of the layers at anytime). **Set** it as the **current layer**.

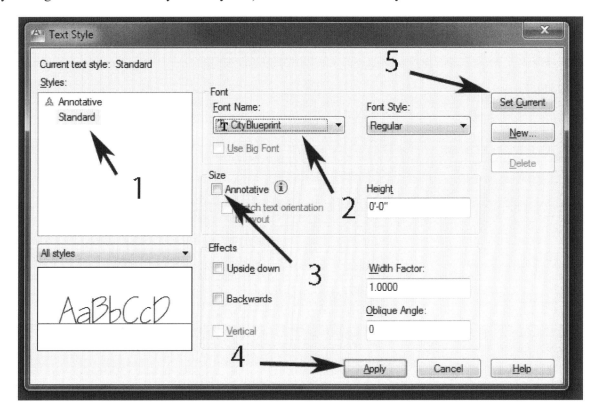

Fig 1-59

Type: **style <e>**. The **Text Style** dialog box will open as in **Fig 1-59**. Click on **Standard** (1 in Fig 1-59). In the window at **Font Name** (2 in Fig 1-59) scroll to **City Blueprint** and click. **Uncheck the Annotative** box. Click **Apply** (4) (if the **Apply** box is not highlighted then skip this step), then **Set Current** (5), and **Close**.

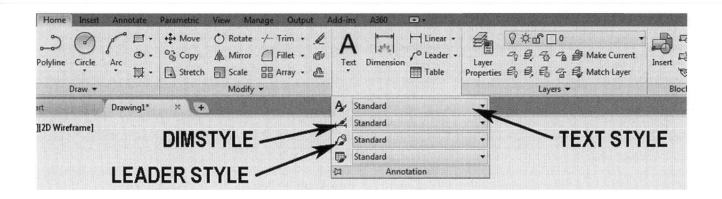

If you hover over the icons it will reveal their names.

Fig 1-60A

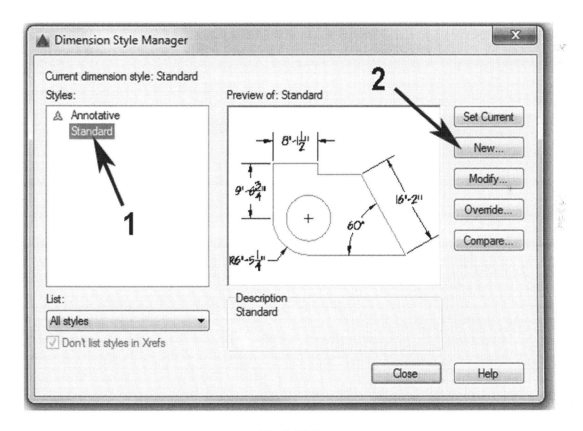

Fig 1-60B

Click on the **Dimension Style** button by clicking on the down arrow at the bottom of the **Annotation** palette next to the word Annotation (or type **dimstyle**). A dialog box will open. **Select** the **Standard** style as shown in **Fig 1-60A**. **Click New (Fig 1-60B)**. When the **Create New Dimension Style** box appears **name** this new style **Quarter**. Then click on **Continue**. **The New Dimension Style: Quarter** box shown in **Fig 1-61** will appear.

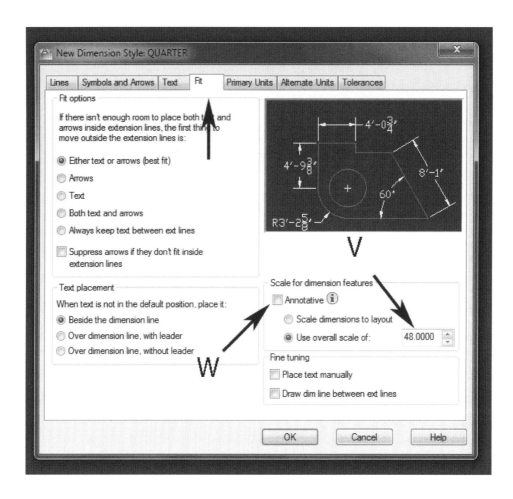

Fig 1-61

Click on the **Fit tab**. In the box that says: **Use Overall Scale of:** (**V** in **Fig 1-61**) highlight the number in the box (double clicking on it) and overtype it with **48**. Make sure the **Annotative is turned off** at **W** in Fig 1-61.

Click the **Primary Units** tab and make sure that **Architectural** is displayed in the **Unit Format** window.

Click on the Symbols and Arrows tab and in the Arrowheads window select Architectural tick. This should automatically change the second to read the same but if not then set it to Architectural tick in the second window also.

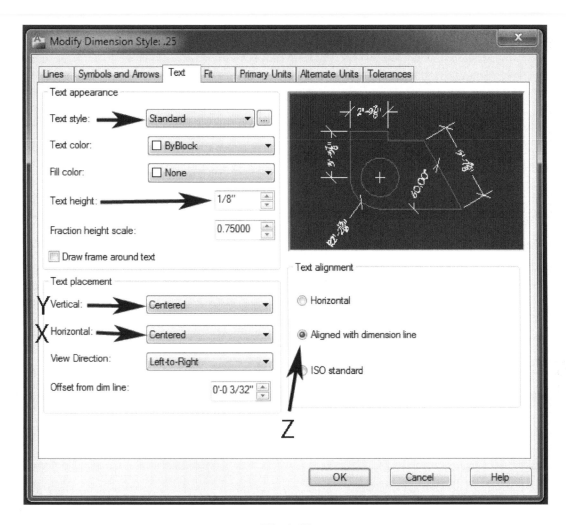

Fig 1-62

Click on the **Text** tab at the top of the box (Fig 1-62). Make certain that **Standard** appears in the **Text Style** window. Set the **Text height** to **1/8"**.Then below in the **Text Placement** box open the **Horozontal** drop down menu (**X** in **Fig 1-62**) and click on **Centered**. In the **Vertical** box (**Y**) select **Centered**. Turn on the button for: **Aligned with dimension line** (**Z**). Click **OK**.

Back at the **Dimension Style** box click on the **Quarter**, then **Set Current**, and **Close**.

In architectural design it is common to have the text (the dimension) above the line, but here we are centering to keep the drawings more compact so that these drawings will print out on a home/office printer.

This setup is for a dimension style using a quarter inch to the foot scale (¼" = 1').

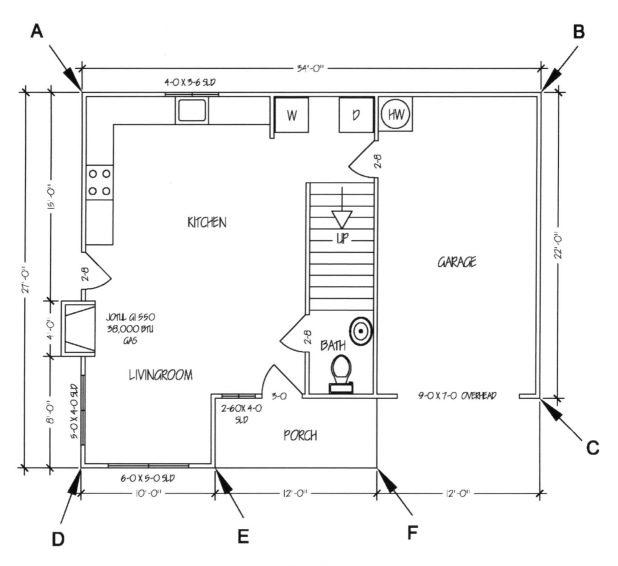

Fig 1-63

Now click on the **Linear** button on the **Dimensions** palette (on the Annotate ribbon co-located with Aligned, Angular, Arc Length, Radius, Diameter, Jogged and Ordinate—it could read any of these—click on the down arrow to see the list or type: dimlinear). Turn the **Object Snap on** and snap to the upper left corner of the building (**A** in **Fig 1-63**). Now snap to the upper right corner (**B**) of the building and move the mouse up. When the dimension line is approximately where you see it in Fig 1-63 **click** and it will set it in place. Keep these dimensions close to the building if you want to be able to print this out on a 8.5 x 11 paper (it just fits). You may want to move the kitchen window text—4-0 x 3-6 SLD—closer to the building first.

Now repeat this process on the garage wall to the right. **Click Linear** then point **B** then **C** in **Fig 1-63**, pull it out to the right, and **click** to set it in place.

You must be careful to **Osnap to the corner** of the building and **not to the end of the dimension indicator**. If you get a weird measurement that is probably what is happening. Zoom in if needed to differentiate.

Click on the **Linear** command and then click on the front of the living room, snap to the lower left corner of the building first (**D**) and then to the corner of the 10 ft pop out section (**E**). Pull it down and **set it** with a **click**. Now **click** on the **Continue** button on the **Dimensions palette** (co-located with the Baseline button) and snap to the corner of the porch (**F**). **Do not enter or right click**. Continue on and snap to the outside corner of the garage (**C**) then <e>.

You should see the dimensions shown in **Fig 1-63**. This is the continuous tool that automatically aligns a string of dimensions.

At the left side use the **Linear** command to create the 8'-0" as shown in Fig 1-63, then the **Continue** button to create the 4'-0" and the 15'0". Use the **Linear** button to create the 27' dimension.

The Continue command saves you from having to click the Linear repeatedly when there is a continuous line of dimensions and it lines them up perfectly.

Congratulations you have finished the first floor plans!

2nd Story Floor Plan

It is not necessary that you draw the second story floor plans. The dimensions and information that you need to continue this course are provided so that you can complete the chapters without drawing the second story.

If you want to draw the second story floor plans look at the completed plans in Appendix IV, and repeat the steps in this chapter. The Index identifies where to find all of the necessary commands and processes if you forget how you did something.

If you are going to draw the second story floor plan, use the copy that you made of the drawing (Fig 1-15) and **make a new copy**. You will need more copies of this for other views later.

A Few Notes

Here you have a completed floor plan and you now know a lot about how to use AutoCAD for drawing in two dimensions. There are a number of different ways to draw any particular object in AutoCAD. None of them are wrong. Readers of this book will develop their own style of drawing as time goes on. Some of what I have demonstrated here is not the easiest or fastest (or best) way, but rather the easiest to explain. The idea is to get you drawing what you need as quickly as possible and then you can fine tune your methods as you go along. Alternate methods for many of these techniques will be discussed as we go along.

Remember that all the commands can be typed in (as opposed to using the mouse and clicking buttons).

Take some time and look at the **Options** dialog box. Type options and <e>. Here you will find dozens of settings for many parts of the system. You can change the size or shape of the pick boxes for example. You can set the default for something other than inches (feet perhaps). You can set the default for line weight. Lots of options, most of which you will never need, but it is good to know what is available in case you find yourself looking for some esoteric setting.

Remember to **save your work often** as you draw. It is a (minor) tragedy to lose hours of work because of some strange computer glitch. Name this file **Paradise** (the fictional street name of our project) and save it to your computer. The desktop is a good place if you are going to be going at this course intensively.

There is an automatic save function find it in the **Options** dialog box (type **options**), then the **Open and Save** tab. Check the box next to **Automatic save** and set the **time between saves**—not too often because the program freezes while it saves your work—20 minutes is a good compromise. Check the box next to **Create backup copy with each save.**

Explore using right clicks as you draw. Use it to repeat commands and enter. Right clicks do a variety of things so the best way to learn about this is to right click at each stage of any process to see what happens.

Chapter 2—Elevations

2.1 Story Pole

If you completed Chapter 1 you have acquired many of the skills that you need to draw with AutoCAD. I will not repeat the individual steps to perform the functions that you have already learned (Line, Rectangle, Move, etc.). For much of the elevation drawing you will be instructed simply to draw what you see in a particular figure. Only new skills will be fully detailed. If you have forgotten how to do something look in the **Index** for the location of the instructions for each command.

> **All the drawing in this book is performed in one file.** If you are reopening AutoCAD, then select your Paradise file (that you saved from Chapter 1) from the menu under the File tab. In other words: **do not create (open) a new file for each chapter**.

> Remember that we are using the shorthand symbol **<e>** to represent pressing the **enter** key on your keyboard.

Look at the completed elevations in Appendix IV. These are the elevations for this house. In this chapter we will draw the east elevation shown here (this is the front of the house that faces the street).

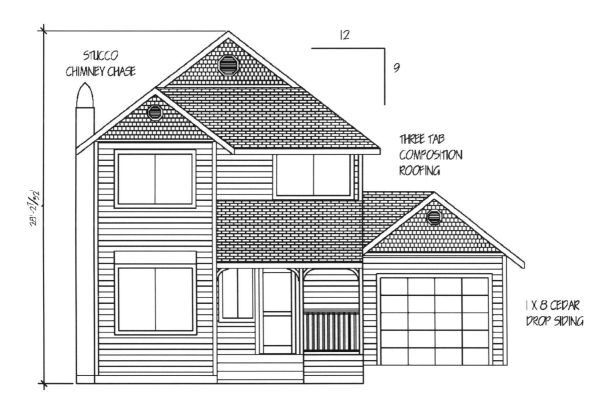

A good place to start when drawing elevations is to **create** a **story pole line**. This is a reference that defines the various elevation levels of the structure: the exterior ground level, the floor levels, the top of wall levels, etc. Fig 2-1 depicts the story pole for this design.

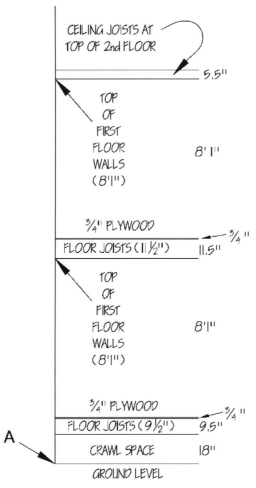

CEILING JOISTS AT TOP OF 2nd FLOOR — 5.5"

TOP OF FIRST FLOOR WALLS (8'1") — 8'1"

¾" PLYWOOD — ¾"
FLOOR JOISTS (11½") — 11.5"

TOP OF FIRST FLOOR WALLS (8'1") — 8'1"

¾" PLYWOOD — ¾"
FLOOR JOISTS (9½") — 9.5"

A → CRAWL SPACE — 18"

GROUND LEVEL

Fig. 2-1

First, create a new **Layer**, make it **orange** in color and name it **Construction**. **Set it current**.

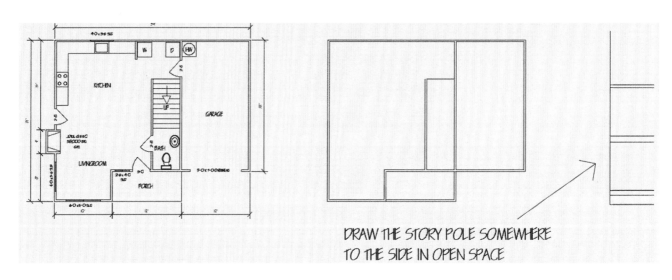

DRAW THE STORY POLE SOMEWHERE TO THE SIDE IN OPEN SPACE

Fig 2-2A

Zoom out and **pan** to the right of your drawing as in **Fig 2-2A**. The exact placement is not important—anywhere in open space will work. With the **Ortho on** draw a **vertical line 34 ft** long.

Now **draw** the **horizontal lines** shown in **Fig 2-1**. Make them **8 ft** long. Draw **line A** (make it 8' long) at the bottom, then use **Offset** to create the other horizontal lines. The **offset measurements between each line**, starting at the bottom, are as follows: **18 / 9.5 / .75 / 8'1 / 11.5 / .75 / 8'1 / 5.5**. These are the measurements from line to line—*not from line* **A** in Fig 2-1.

Fig 2-1 details what each measurement represents. Starting at the bottom moving upward, the 18" at the bottom is the **crawl space**, above that is the 9.5" height of the **floor joists**, above that is the ¾" **plywood** subfloor, next the 8'1" represents the distance between the floor and the **first story ceiling**, etc.

Draw a 14' line at the top of the story pole as in Fig 2-3A.

TURN ME OFF

Fig 2-2B

Turn off the **Text layer** and the **Dimension layer**. To do this go to the **Layer Control** window and click on the **little light bulb** next to the **Text Layer** (see **Fig 2-2B**) and again next to the dimension layer. When you do this the text and dimensions will disappear (we will bring it back later). You cannot turn off the current layer.

At the top of the Story Pole draw a **horizontal line** to the right **14'** long **(Fig 2-3A)**.

Copy the **first story floor plan** to the end of the **14'** line as in **Fig 2-3A**. Use **Copy** and select the **lower left corner** osnap icon of the floor plan as the **base point**. Read the prompts at the command line. Snap this to the endpoint of the top horizontal line (14' line) as in **Fig 2-3A**.

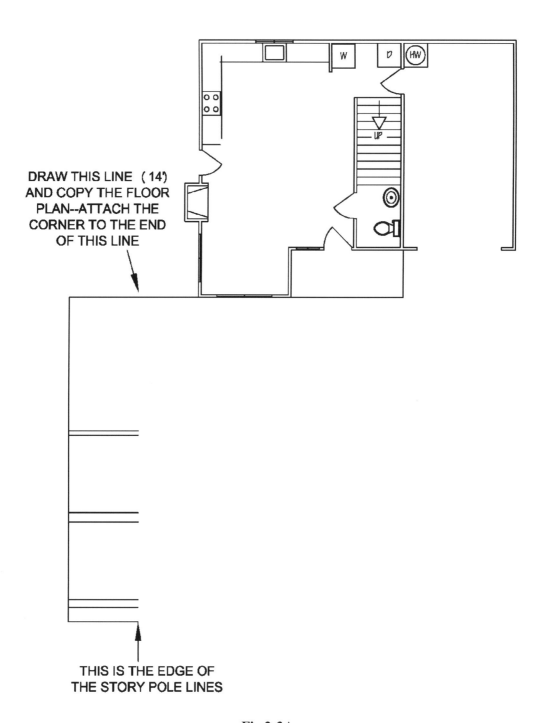

DRAW THIS LINE (14')
AND COPY THE FLOOR
PLAN--ATTACH THE
CORNER TO THE END
OF THIS LINE

THIS IS THE EDGE OF
THE STORY POLE LINES

Fig 2-3A

Select the **0 Layer** from the **Layer Control** window. Draw the **lines** shown in **Fig 2-3B**.

Draw the **horizontal lines** first as you see in **Fig 2-3B**. Draw them with the **Line** tool. Attach the starting point to the appropriate end of the story pole line then, with the **Ortho on**, end them in the space to the right of the floor plan—don't worry about the exact length as we will trim them back later. Make them extra long so they end well beyond the floor plan (we will trim them back later). Just click in open space for the second point of each line. Now add the vertical lines. As you can see the **vertical lines** are **drawn down from**: the **exterior corners** of the floor plan, the **edges and centers of the windows**, and the **sides of the doors**.

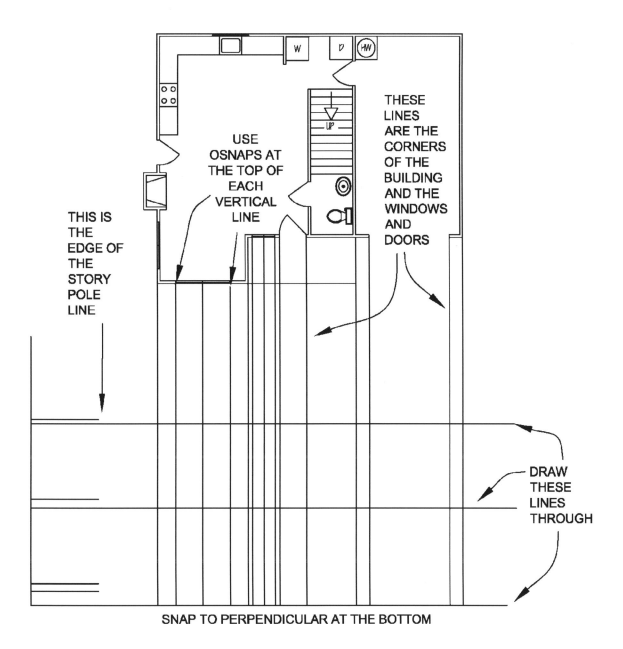

Fig. 2-3B

Use the **Object Snap** to attach the lines at the top (at the floor plan). With the **Ortho on** draw the lines down and attach them to the **Perpendicular Osnap** icon at the bottom.

We are using the floor plan as a template to measure the lines for the elevation (You could just use measurements to get the same results, but this is faster). If you have trouble understanding what we are doing look ahead at the figures to see how the drawing develops.

The vertical lines that we drew down from the windows and doors represent the windows and doors of the *first story* (the second story will be added later), so we will **trim** these lines at the **top** of the **first story** elevation and separate them from the second story as in Fig 2-4. **Trim** them to **line B** in **Fig 2-4**. Leave the corners as in Fig 2-4.

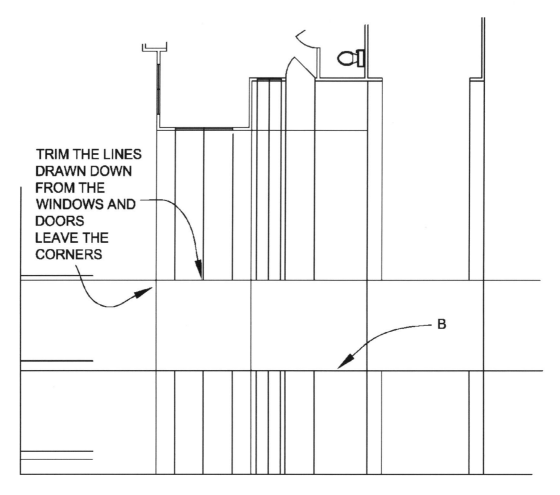

TRIM THE LINES DRAWN DOWN FROM THE WINDOWS AND DOORS LEAVE THE CORNERS

B

Fig 2-4

Now let's draw the line for the top of the doors and windows. It is offset down from the ceiling line (**B** in **Fig 2-4**). Use **Offset** and draw a line **14.5** inches **down** from line **B** (the top of the wall line) to create line **C** in **Fig 2-5**. **Trim** the lines at the **X**'s in **Fig. 2-5**.

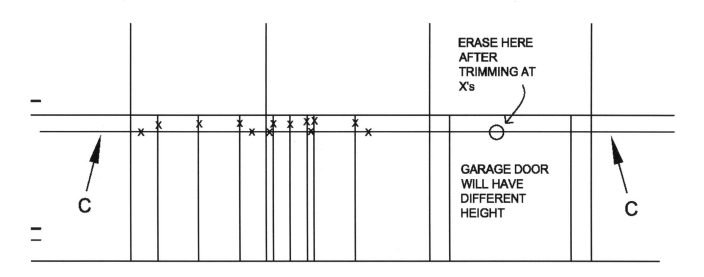

Fig. 2-5

Once trimmed you will see the **top line** and **sides** of the first story **windows** and **doors**. Your drawing will look like Fig 2-6. Look ahead a few figures and it is clear what we are doing.

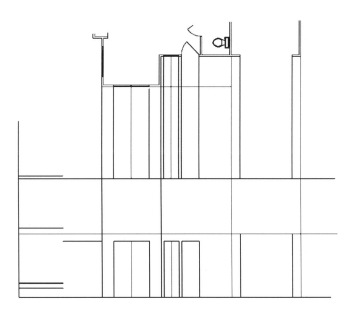

Fig 2-6

Now draw the **bottom** line of the **windows** using **Offset** as in **Fig 2-7**. The big window is **5** ft tall the small is **4** ft. The **bottom** of the **door** is drawn from the **plywood line** of the **story pole** (the bottom of the door is the ¾" **plywood line** on the story pole). **Trim** the lines from the corners and **Erase** everything else until you see **Fig 2-7**. Leave the line shown in Fig 2-7 as a marker.

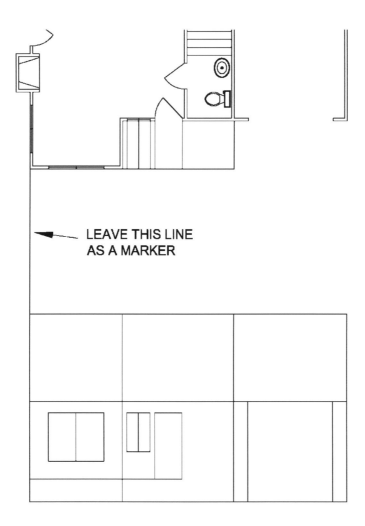

LEAVE THIS LINE
AS A MARKER

Fig 2-7

This is all of the information that we can obtain form the first story floor plan. **Erase** this copy of the **1ˢᵗ floor plan.** If you have drawn the second story floor plan then **place** the **second story floor plan** in its place as in **Fig 2-8**. Copy the second story floor plan as shown in Fig 2-8.

You do not need to draw the second story floor plan. Follow the directions.

If you have not drawn the second story floor plan, all you need are the six lines that delineate the sides of the windows shown in **Fig 2-8**. Use the information indicated in Fig 2-8A. Look ahead at the figures to see what we are doing.

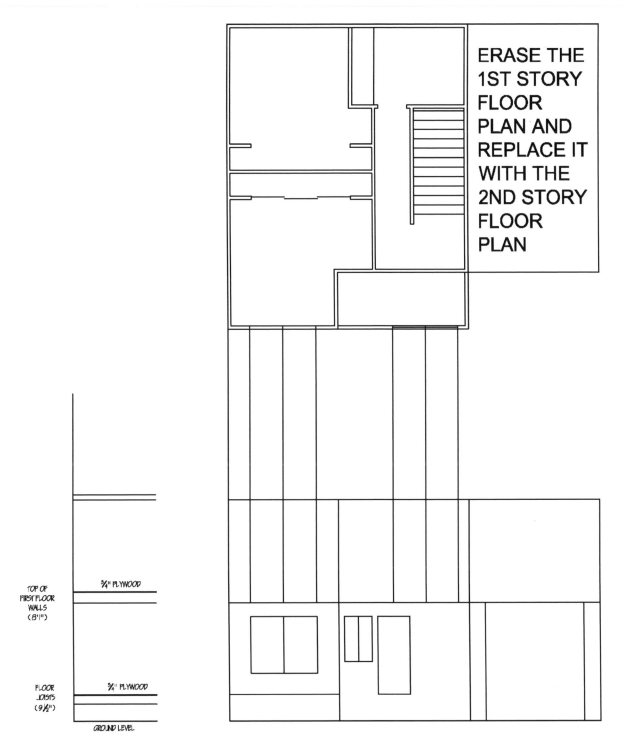

ERASE THE 1ST STORY FLOOR PLAN AND REPLACE IT WITH THE 2ND STORY FLOOR PLAN

TOP OF FIRST FLOOR WALLS (8'1")

¾" PLYWOOD

FLOOR JOISTS (9½")

¾" PLYWOOD

GROUND LEVEL

Fig. 2-8

Line D (the vertical line is line D) is **12 inches from E**. Use **Offset** from the corner (E) to create D. Then **offset** again **3'** to create the next line to the left, and again (**3' offset**) to create the next line from that. The window is 6'-0" as shown in **Fig 2-8A**.

The **three lines marked F** in **Fig 2-8A** can be drawn up from the first story window lines below as they are in the same lateral position as the first story window (We could have left them from the first story, but we are doing it this way to demonstrate the concept).

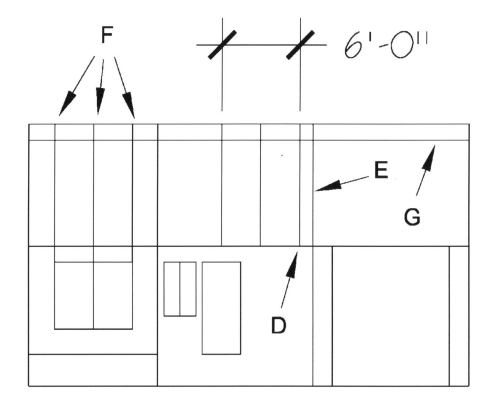

Fig 2-8A

After you draw the lines for the second story windows as in Fig 2-8, create a top of window **line** (**G in Fig 2-8A**). It is **14.5** inches below the top of the second story wall line as shown in **Fig 2-8A**. **Trim** these windows as before and use the **Offset** to create the **bottom line** of the **windows**. (4' for the window on the left and 3'4" for the window on the right).

Now add the **lines** for the garage as in **Fig 2-9**. Use **Offset 2'** and **7'** as indicated. **Trim** at the **X**'s and then **erase** at the **O**'s.

Look at the completed drawing at the beginning of this chapter if you need a reference as to what the various lines represent (or flip forward through the Figures to see the progression).

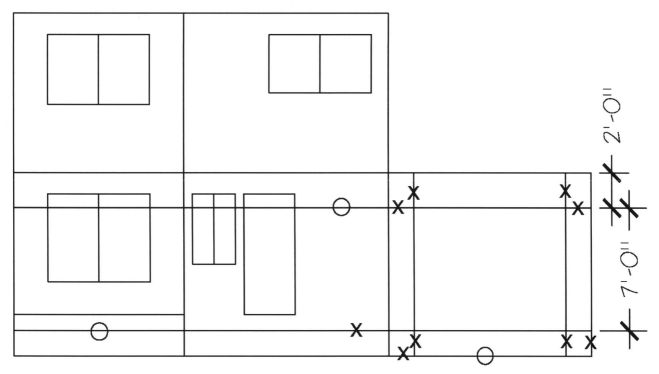

Fig 2-9

Trim the lines to look like **Fig 2-9A**.

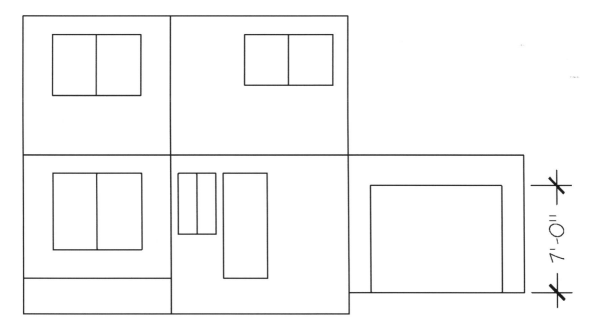

Fig 2-9A

Move the **story pole** away from this drawing so it doesn't crowd the elevation drawing. You will use it for some of the other drawings.

2.2 The Roof Lines

I like to draw a graphic of the roof where it meets the wall. It is a good way to establish precise rooflines. **Draw** the figure in **Fig 2-10** somewhere in empty space to the right of the elevation. Use **four separate lines** (*not the rectangle tool*).This represents the **wall** that the rafters sit on.

Fig 2-10

Turn on the **Object Snap** and turn off the **Ortho**. Click **Line** and then click on point **H** in **Fig 2-10** (*do not enter*). Now **type: @20'<37 <e>**. You will see a line appear that is twenty feet long at an angle of 37 degrees as in Fig 2-11. Thirty-seven degrees is the angle of our roof slope (9 in 12 slope in construction terms).

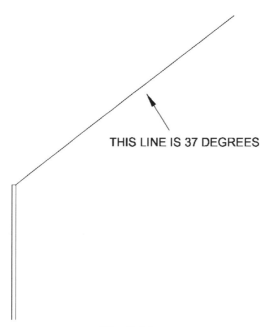

Fig. 2-11

Now we will draw Fig 2-12. Look at **Fig 2-12** then **read** through the **steps** in Figures 2-12A through 2-12D.

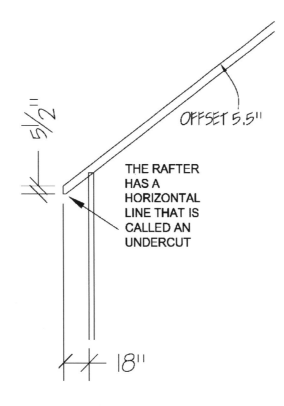

Fig. 2-12

First, **Offset** the **angled line** by **5.5"** as in **Fig 2-12A**.

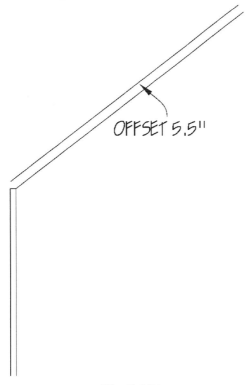

Fig. 2-12A

Use **Offset** to draw the line that is **18"** to the left of the wall in **Fig 2-12B**.

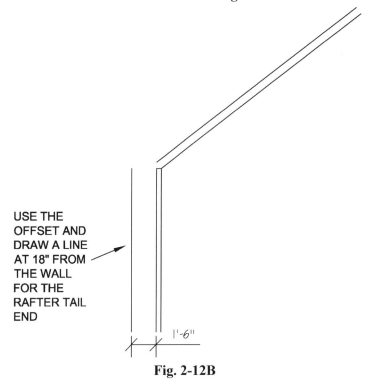

USE THE
OFFSET AND
DRAW A LINE
AT 18" FROM
THE WALL
FOR THE
RAFTER TAIL
END

1'-6"

Fig. 2-12B

Extend the **angled lines** to meet this 18" offset line as in **Fig 12-2C**.

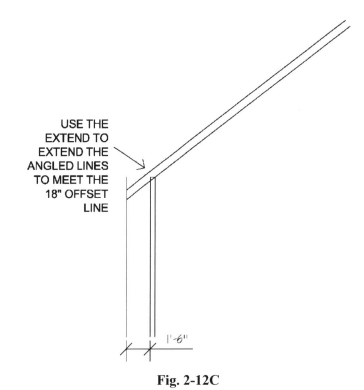

USE THE
EXTEND TO
EXTEND THE
ANGLED LINES
TO MEET THE
18" OFFSET
LINE

1'-6"

Fig. 2-12C

Click on the **Line** button then hold down the shift button on your keyboard and right click the mouse. Select **From** then **click** on the **point** indicated in **Fig 2-12D** then **hover** (*do not click*) over the icon at the bottom of this line, **type 5.5 <e>**, this will attach the **first point** of a new line to this vertical line. **Draw** the line out to the **right** (Ortho on) and **click** in open space to create the line shown in **Fig 2-12D**.

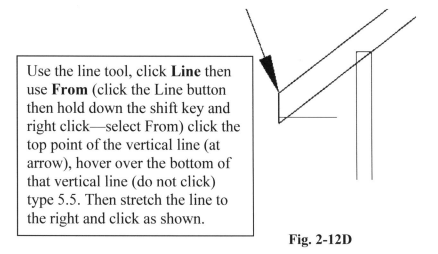

Use the line tool, click **Line** then use **From** (click the Line button then hold down the shift key and right click—select From) click the top point of the vertical line (at arrow), hover over the bottom of that vertical line (do not click) type 5.5. Then stretch the line to the right and click as shown.

Fig. 2-12D

Trim the end of the rafter to look like **Fig 2-13**.

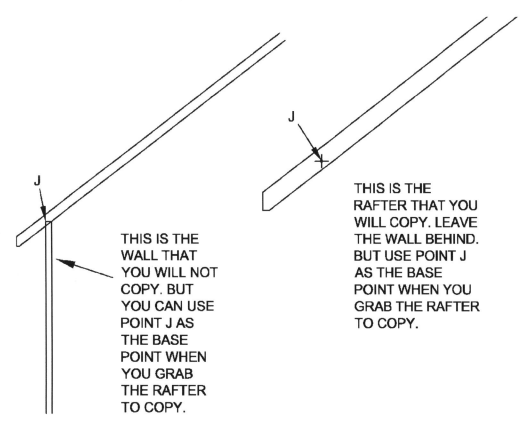

J

THIS IS THE WALL THAT YOU WILL NOT COPY. BUT YOU CAN USE POINT J AS THE BASE POINT WHEN YOU GRAB THE RAFTER TO COPY.

J

THIS IS THE RAFTER THAT YOU WILL COPY. LEAVE THE WALL BEHIND. BUT USE POINT J AS THE BASE POINT WHEN YOU GRAB THE RAFTER TO COPY.

Fig. 2-13

Copy the roof **rafter** but **not the wall**. Read the prompts in the Command Line window. When it says: **Specify base point**, **click** on the upper wall corner at **J**, and **snap it** to **point K** on the elevation drawing as in **Fig 2-14**.

You will notice that the base point (for copying, moving, etc) need not be part of the items to be copied. The base point can be anywhere on the screen (point J in this case). This is very useful for many applications. In this case point J represents the top outside corner of the wall; the rafter has a notch (called a bird's mouth cut or seat cut) that sits on the corner of the wall frame.

One of the concepts in AutoCAD that is difficult to explain is: when you **copy (or move, rotate, etc)**, the **point at which you grab** the object to be copied **does not need to be copied** with the object. This is called the base point.

In the example of the rafter in Fig 2-13, we are **copying only** the **object shown to the right** (minus the cross that represents the cursor), but we are using **point J** (the intersection of the horizontal and vertical wall lines) as a **base point** (the point where we grab the object to be copied). This is the point we wish to snap to the new destination point of the copy (as at K in Fig 2-14).

This same principle applies to the Move command, Rotate, any command that requires a base point.

The base point for these commands can be anywhere in the workspace.

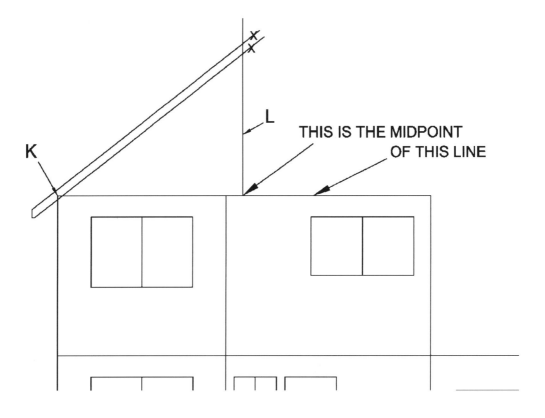

Fig 2-14

Find the center of the top wall line as in **Fig 2-14** and draw a **line** straight up (L) with the **Ortho on**. End the line in open space above the rafter (just click the end of this line in open space). **Trim** the rafter at the **X**'s shown in **Fig 2-14**.

Now click the **Mirror** button on the Modify palette and **select** the **rafter** (only the rafter)—*do not select the top of the wall*. **Enter** and **read** the command line **prompt**. It asks for the first point of the mirror line. Click the **bottom** and **then** the **top** of **line L** <enter>. You will see Fig 2-15.

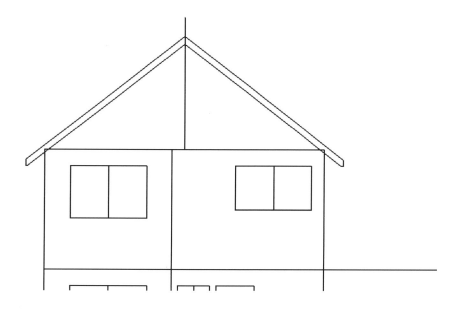

Fig. 2-15

Now **repeat** the process to **create Fig 2-16**. You can click on the center of the window for the first point of the mirror line (you do not need to actually draw a line with the line tool—the **mirror line** is an invisible line drawn between **any two points** you choose to click on). Use **Ortho, click** on **Mirror**, then **select** the **rafter** to the left <e>, **click** on the **middle** of the **window** and then **click anywhere above** the drawing (anywhere in the open space for the upper end of the mirror line).

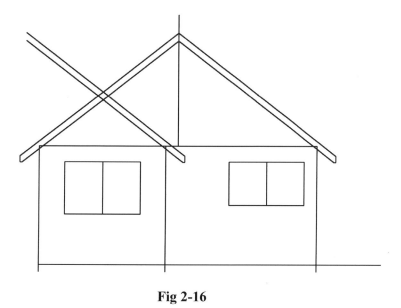

Fig 2-16

Mirror lines are not lines drawn on the screen. Mirror lines are a boundary between the two mirrored images. See Appendix I—Mirror for an explanation of this concept.

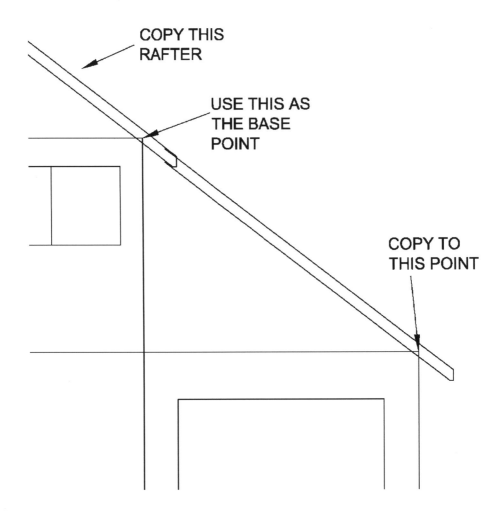

COPY THIS
RAFTER

USE THIS AS
THE BASE
POINT

COPY TO
THIS POINT

Fig. 2-16A

Copy the rafter to the right side of the garage (**Fig 2-16A**). Now draw the roof on the garage using the mirror tool. Use the **midpoint of the top line** of the **garage door** as the **mirror** line. Start the mirror line at **M** in **Fig. 2-17** and draw the line straight up with the **Ortho on**—**click** in the open space **above** for the upper end of the mirror line.

Draw a **line** from the top of **T** in **Fig 2-17** to the left and attach it to the vertical line of the house as shown.

Trim line **L** (Fig 2-14) **above** and **below** the **rafters** to look like **Fig 2-17**.

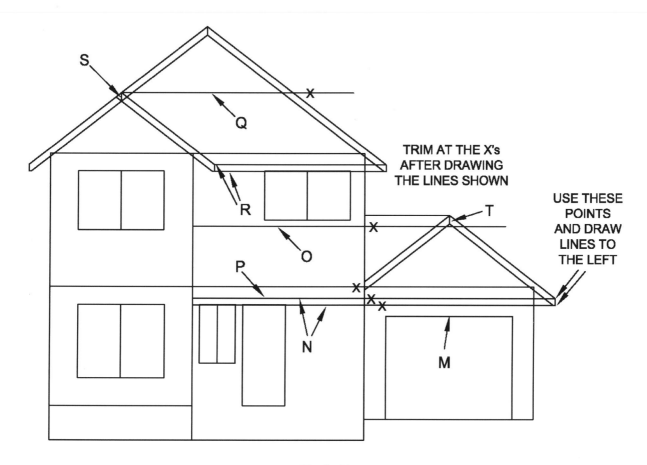

Fig 2-17

Draw the fascia **lines** of the front porch roof (**N in Fig 2-17**) using the garage roof overhang as a template as shown in Fig 2-17. Draw the **line** at the top of the porch roof (**O**) with the **Offset** tool at **4'11"** from line **P**.

Draw **line Q**. Start the line at the small ridge shown in Fig 2-17 and draw it through into open space (no object snap at the right end of this line). Then **trim** it at the **X** shown. Draw the **lines** for the fascia for this roof section by connecting the overhangs as shown at **R**. Add **lines S** and **T**. Then **trim** at the **X**'s. **Trim** and **erase** to look like **Fig 2-18**. You will see a house.

Fig 2-18

That was a lot of steps. Don't worry if your drawing is not exact, or if you missed a trim here or there. You can trim and add lines later. The idea is to learn how to draw, not to create a perfect copy of this drawing.

2.3 Porch

Next we will add the front porch posts. First draw the **line** for the porch deck (the floor) as in **Fig 2-19**; it is ¾" **below** the **bottom** of the **door**.

> The exact locations and sizes are not really important; we are learning drawing techniques and not trying to create a perfect drawing. So don't spend too much energy trying to be super precise at this point in the process. For now it is best to move along as quickly as possible in order to learn the drawing techniques. You can make your drawings precise after you learn how to draw.

Use **Offset** to establish line **U** in **Fig 2-19** it is offset **5'2"** from the (corner) line **V**. Use **Offset** again to create the **lines** marked **W** (there are two lines W—these represent the width of the posts for the porch—look ahead in the figures to see what these lines represent) these are the porch posts. They are **offset 3.5"** from **U** on the left and **3.5"** from **V** on the right as shown. Then **trim** at the **X**'s and **erase** at the **O**'s to **see Fig 2-20**. Look at the completed drawing on page 51 to see what this should look like.

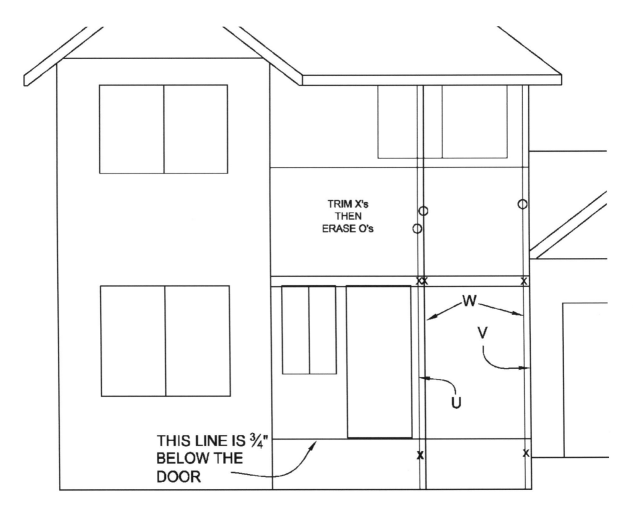

Fig 2-19

If you zoom way in and look at the top of the door and the window next to the door you will see that the lines cross over the porch fascia. **Trim** them back to line **Y** in Fig **2-20**.

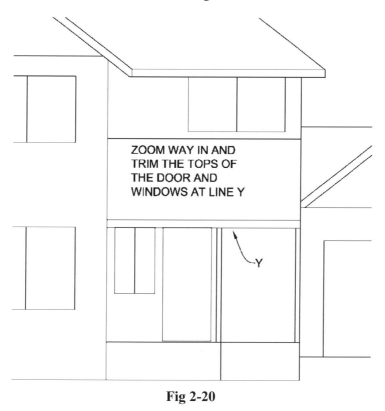

Fig 2-20

2.4 Knee Braces

Now we are going to do something a bit more complicated: draw the knee braces on the porch (Fig 2-21).

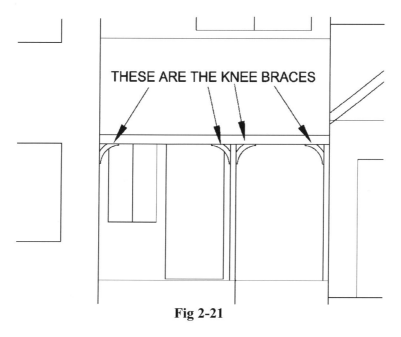

Fig 2-21

Fig 2-22 shows the steps for drawing a knee brace. Off to the side of the elevation—in open space, draw the first **rectangle** at **13" x 13"**. Use the **rectangle** tool. You must click the screen at the end to set the rectangle.

Now click the **Circle** button on the Draw palette and click at the point shown as **A** in **Fig 2-22**. Follow the prompts at the Command Line. It asks for a **radius** or diameter—select radius). Type **12 <e>**. **Trim** and **erase** as shown to get **FIG B**.

Use **Offset** to make another larger arc (3" offset) as in **FIG C** in **Fig 2-22**. **Trim** as shown to get **FIG D**.

Add a **Point** to the corner **E**. **Click** on **Point** (same as Multiple Points) on the **Draw** palette (click the down arrow next to Draw or type point) and then **click** on the corner **E**. This point is called a **Node** when we snap to it. **Trim** the knee brace to get **FIG E**. *Your point at E will be very small*.

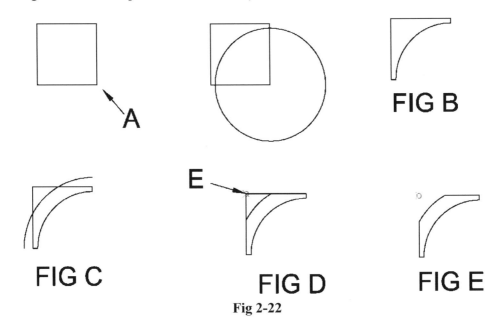

Fig 2-22

Copy this knee brace. The **base point** (where you grab it) is at the **node** point **E** that you created. First you must go to the **Osnap** settings and select the **Node Osnap**: right click in the Osnap button at the bottom of your screen, select settings and turn on the Node Osnap (See Appendix I—Object snap settings for help). **Copy** the knee brace to points **F** and **G** in **Fig 2-23** using the node at point E as the base point for the knee brace.

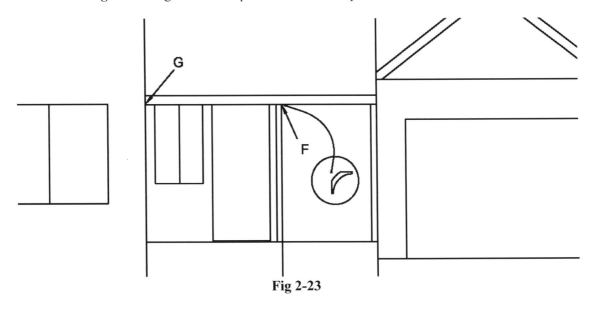

Fig 2-23

Make a **copy** of the **knee brace** in open work space. Include the point/node in this copy. Use the **Mirror** command to create a **mirror image** (see Appendix I—Mirror if you need help). **Copy** the mirror image knee brace to the other two **inside corner points** to get **Fig 2-21**. These are the intersections of the lines that represent the posts—not the door or the outside corner of the porch.

2.5 Gable Vents

We will now draw the gable vents. Click on the **Polygon** button on the **Draw** palette (co-located with Rectangle). The command line will ask for the **number** of **sides**. Type **8 <e>**. Off to the side of our drawing a bit, in open space as in **Fig 2-24, click**, you will see nothing, but the Command line will read: **Enter an option…** the default is **Inscribed (I)** so just hit the **<e>** to select this option. Now it asks for the **radius**, type **9 <e>**. An octagon will appear where you clicked in the open space. **Make** a **copy** of this (so you have two).

We are going to scale down one of these copies of the octagon. Click on the **Scale** button on the **Modify** palette. **Select** the **copy** of the **octagon** and **<e>**. The **base point** can be anywhere in the octagon, **click**. Type **.66 <e>**. This will now be 2/3 (66% or .66) of the original copy.

Draw the **lines** in **Fig 2-24** down from the **bottom** of the ridges. **Copy** the large octagon to the bottom of the **18"** line and the smaller octagon to the **12"** lines as in **Fig 2-25**.

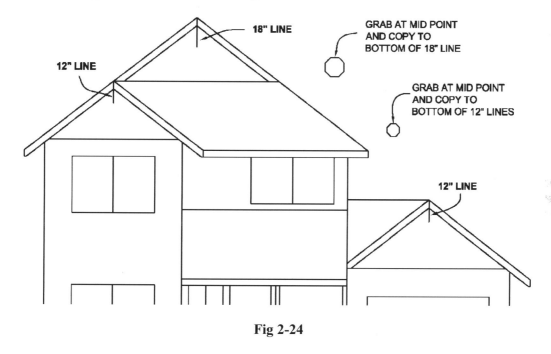

Fig 2-24

2.6 Trim

Let's put some trim on the building. Draw **line H** at the bottom of **Fig 2-25**. Offset it **7.5"** from **I**. Trim it at the **X**. This is the bottom of the siding.

Draw the **lines J** (there are three). **Offset** this from the existing gable lines **2.5** inches, below for the garage and small gable, and above for the large upper gable. **Extend** these lines to meet the vertical lines at the edge of the building (see **Fig 2-25**).

Offset the corners **4"**, and **Extend** these **lines** up to meet the lines **J**.

Offset the windows to the outside **4"** to create the window trim. **Offset** the front **door** and the **garage door 4"** to the **outside**.

Use **Fillet** (set radius to **0"**) to close up the **corners** of the window and door trim. Read the prompts. Make sure you catch the **third prompt** and enter **M** for multiple. That way you don't have to restart the command for each corner.

Extend the window **trim** next to the **door** over to meet the door trim at **K**. **Extend** the side of the door and the door trim down to the deck at lines **L**.

Offset the octagons by **2"** to the outside. **Trim** at the **X**'s and then **erase** at the **O**'s as shown in **Fig 2-25**.

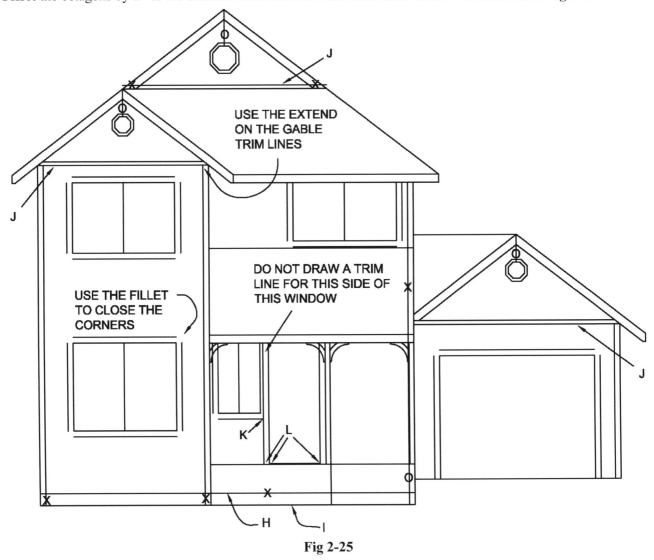

Fig 2-25

Draw the top of the lower left window at **M** in **Fig. 2-26**—this a small roof cap over the box window. The **offset** for this is **12"**. Clean up any loose ends to see Fig 2-26 (minus the grids on the garage door—they are next).

Trim the lines inside the porch **knee braces**.

2.7 Garage Door and Porch Rail

Now we will draw the lines on the garage door.

Type **divide** <e>. **Select** the right side of the garage door <e> (at **N** in **Fig 2-26**). Type **5** <e>. **Read the Command Line** as you do this so you can see what is happening. You are dividing this line into five sections. Each section is marked by a **node** that you will only see if you try to snap something to it (or if you set your nodes to a larger size—see Appendix I—Nodes and Points). Make certain that the **Node Object Snap** is turned **on** in your Osnap settings window.

Click **line** and then attach the **first point** of the line to a **node** on **line N,** draw a line to the left and attach it to the perpendicular osnap on the other side of the garage door (you will need to move your cursor up and down the line N until you locate a node Osnap—the same type of osnap point/node that you used to copy the knee braces at E in Fig 2-22). See **Fig 2-26**. **Repeat** this process for each of the four horizontal lines. Don't mistake the midpoint osnap for a node.

Now **repeat** this process for each of the three vertical lines—use **Divide** then **select** the line (**P**) at the top of the door opening as the **select object**, at the prompt type **4** divisions and <e>. The midpoint and the middle node will be the same point this time—pick either osnap for the center line.

Fig 2-26

Next we will draw the **deck rail**. Look at **Fig 2-32** to see the completed deck rail.

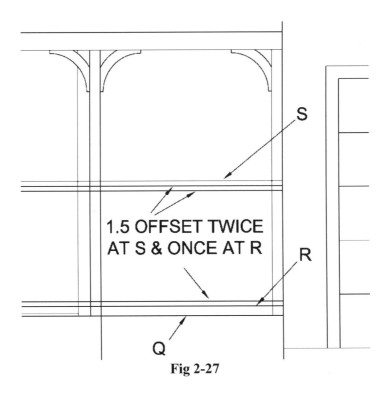

Fig 2-27

Offset the deck line (**Q** in **Fig 2-27**) **3"** to draw line **R**. **Offset Q** again **42"** to create **line S** in **Fig 2-27**. Create the **thickness** of the **rails** (single at the **bottom** and double at the **top rail**) using **1.5 offset** as in **Fig 2-27**.

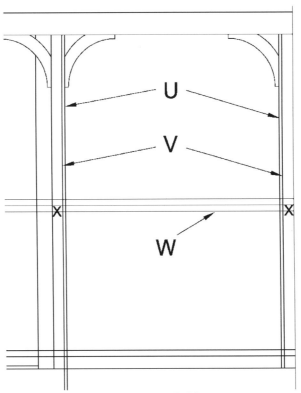

Fig 2-28

Draw **lines V** in **Fig 2-28**. They are **offset .75"** from the lines marked **U**. **Trim** Where you see the **X**'s. This will extend line W beyond lines U by ¾" both sides.

Set the **Construction layer current**.

Type **divide <e>**. **Select** the line **W** in **Fig 2-28**. **Type 11 <e>**. **Set the 0 layer current**.

Now draw lines as you did with the garage door using the **nodes** at the top (line W) and the **perpendicular osnap** at the bottom. **Offset** all of these lines by **.75"** to **both sides** as in **Fig 2-29**. Select all of the middle lines at once and **erase** them. These are the balusters. **Erase** the **V** lines in Fig 2-28. **Trim** the rail lines back to the posts (**U**).

Fig 2-29

There are a number of ways to create rails. We did it this way to demonstrate a method of drawing. It would be faster to create the first baluster and then copy it to the other nodes using the top of the center line as the base point (but not copying the center line).

2.8 Chimney

Draw a line to represent the chimney at **18" offset** from the left exterior wall (see **Y** in **Fig 2-32**). **Click** on the line **Y** and use the **blue grip box** at the top of this line (turn the box red first by clicking on it) to stretch the line up a bit (**do not click** for the **second point**), with the **Ortho on**, then type **30 <e>** (See Appendix I—Line for more on this.). The line will extend upward by 30". **ESC**.

Draw a **line** from the top of this line to the right **18"**. Then draw a **line** down to the rafter. Use the **Ortho**. **Turn off** the **Osnap** and extend the line down below the roof rafter into the open space (random length) then **trim** it back to the roof line.

Let's draw the chimney cap. Draw a **line** from the midpoint of the top of the chimney chase (**Z** in **Fig 2-30**) up **24"**. Offset this line at **5", 7"** and **8"**.

Offset the top line Z of the chimney chase **6" four times**. It should look like **Fig 2-30** without the dimension lines.

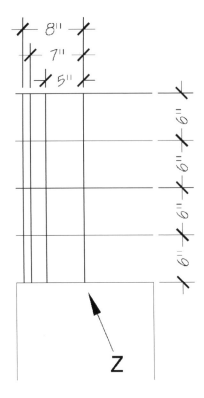

Fig 2-30

Click on the **Spline Fit** button on the **Draw** palette (find it under the little down arrow next to Draw). Turn the **Ortho off**. Turn the **Osnap on**. **Attach** the spline to the points in **Fig. 2-31**. **Start** at the **bottom** and **click** each **successive point up**. After you click the top point **enter**.

Splines can come out with a weird loop or curve at the top. To see how to remedy this, undo the spline and start again. This time, after you click the final point, stretch the spline up and away from the final click point—do not click—move it around until you see the curve that you want and (do not click) **enter** to set the spline. Sometimes the spline will disappear at this point and you will need to enter twice. Occasionally it will not appear even after you enter and you must click on the undo button to make it appear (don't ask).

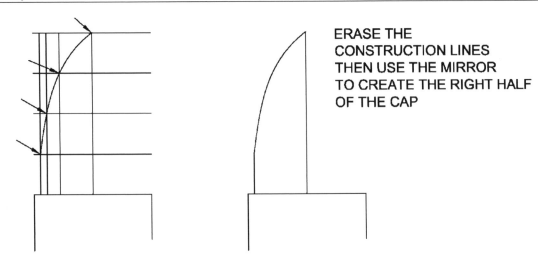

ERASE THE
CONSTRUCTION LINES
THEN USE THE MIRROR
TO CREATE THE RIGHT HALF
OF THE CAP

Fig 2-31

Now use **Mirror** tool and create the other side of the cap (see **Fig 2-32**). Use the center vertical line as the mirror line. **Erase** the center line.

Finish off the chimney chase by drawing **line A** in **Fig 2-32** at the ground level (close off the bottom of the chimney).

Draw in the front steps. Use **8"** and leave the bottom line at **3.5"** to represent the concrete walkway. See **Fig 2-32**.

Clean up the drawings to appear as shown in Fig. 2-32.

Fig 2-32

2.10 Hatch

Now the **Hatch** function will finish off the graphics for this elevation view. Hatch is very useful, but it can be confusing. If you just follow along here you will learn the basic concepts, later we will explore it in more detail.

Set a new layer in the **Layer properties** manager. Name it **Hatch**. Give it a **green** color. Then **Okay**. Back in the main display, select the hatch layer from the drop down menu from **Layer Control** (set it as the current layer).

Click on the **Hatch** button on the **Draw** palette (co-located with Gradient and Boundary). The ribbon shown in Fig 2-33 will appear.

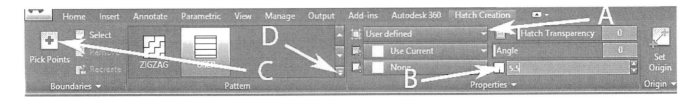

Fig 2-33

Make the following adjustments (follow the letters in Fig 2-33):

   A   Select "User defined" (click the arrow to see the options).
   B   Hatch Spacing: highlight and type in 5.5". (This window identifies as Hatch **Scale** with other settings.)
   C   Click on "Pick points".

In the drawing area, **click at points B** in **Fig 2-34**, then <e>.

Fig 2-34

You should see the horizontal lines in **Fig 2-35**.

Fig 2-35

If you have problems read more in Appendix I—Hatch.

You may have to wait a minute after you click the Add Pick points button: *the cursor needs to become a cross before you can select the pick points.*

Now create the roof hatch and try a few different settings to see how hatch functions.

Click **Hatch**. Select "**Pattern**" at **A** in Fig **2-33** (click the arrow to see the options). **Click** the little down arrow at **D** in **Fig 2-33**. Here you will see a bunch of hatch patterns (Fig 2-36).

Scroll down and look at the patterns. Ar-con is concrete. Ar-sand is sand. Etc. **Select AR-BRSTD** by clicking on it. (AR=BRSTD is actually bricks, but it will work for three tab roofing.) Leave all of the settings as you find them. Click on: **Pick points (C in Fig 2-33)**. In the drawing area click in the roof spaces (**C**) shown in **Fig. 2-35** and **<e>**.

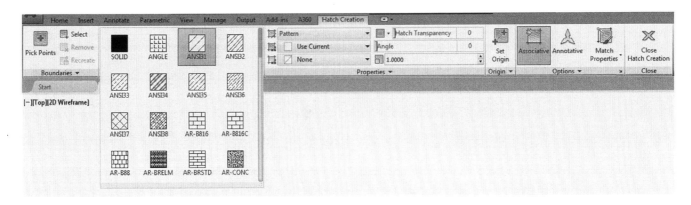

Fig 2-36

Let's play around with the settings a bit to further explore the hatch settings. **Select** the roof hatch (that we just created) by clicking on one of the roof hatch areas (C in Fig 2-35). ***You must click on a hatch when it is highlighted to select it.*** If it is not highlighted at first, then move the cursor around a bit and it should highlight; click to select it (see Appendix I—Hatch if you have problems). **Right click** and **click** on **Hatch Edit** (if you have trouble with this you can type **hatchedit** at the command line). Sometimes this is a bit persnickety and you will have to ESC and start again. When the **Hatch Edit** box opens change the **scale** to **2.000**, then click **OK**. The roof shingles just got huge. You will play around with this setting often when using hatch. Sometimes the scale will be so out of whack that you will see nothing when you OK the hatch. In that case **Undo** and try a different scale. This process will lead you to the right scale.

Do another the **Hatch Edit** on the roof hatch and set the **scale** back to **1**, then **OK**. Or use Undo to get back to the original hatch scale.

Now let's take just a moment to look at a different function. Click on the **Match Properties** button on the **Properties** palette (Home ribbon). The command line reads: **select source object**. The source object is the object whose properties you wish to match. With the pick box (cursor) run over the roof hatch (any section marked C in Fig 2-35) until it lights up and then click on it. A **little paint brush** will **appear** next to the pick box. Now **click** on a section of the siding hatch (any section marked B in Fig 2-34). It will change to a brick hatch like the roof. **ESC** and **Undo** and **change** it **back** to the **siding pattern** (Undo will revert it to the siding hatch pattern).

Match Properties is very useful.

Let's finish up the hatches. Click **Hatch** again. Click **pattern** and then the little box next to the pattern window as before. From the drop down menu choose **AR-B88**. Set the **scale** at **.5**. The **Pick points** now are the three gable ends outside of the octagons at **F** in **Fig 3-37**.

Fig 2-37

These are shingles on the gable ends.

One more Hatch and we are done. Open the **Hatch** dialog box. This time select the **"User defined"** option. In the **Scale** window type **1.5**. For the selection of the **Pick points** click on the **insides of the octagons** (all three), <e>. Look at **Fig 2-38** for the results of all this hatch work.

2.11 Text and Dimensions

That is it for the Front Elevation graphics. We need a few **notes** as in **Fig 2-38**. Select the **Text layer** in the **Layer Control** (the layer we created in Chapter One). **Turn it on** (little light bulb). Use **mtext** and **9"** for the height of the text. Use **bold**. If the text comes out wrong then type style and check to make certain that the **Style 9** is selected—set it current. You can also set this style after you open the Mtext box—set it in the **Text Formatting** bar that opens at the top (to open it type: mtexttoolbar and set the value to 1) or use the ribbon. Add the notes you see in Fig 2-38.

We want an overall height dimension. Select the dimension layer from the Layer control.

Set the Dimension layer current. Turn it on (little light bulb). **Click** on the **Dimension Style** button on the **Annotation** palette (click the down arrow next to Annotation). Make certain that you have the **Quarter** style selected, then press **Set Current** and **Close.**

Click the **linear** button on the **Annotation** or **Dimensions** (it is located on both) palette and then the points shown in **Fig 2-38** (the bottom of the chimney and the peak of the roof).

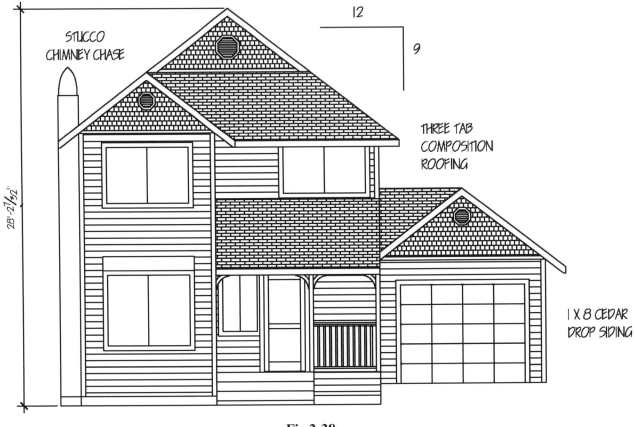

Fig 2-38

Mine reads 28' 2 7/32". That is a bit cumbersome. Let's round it up to the nearest inch.

Click on the **dimension** (click on the number—called the **text**—of the dimension). When the **blue grip boxes** appear **right click**. In the **drop down box** that appears select **Properties**. The **Properties** box will appear as in **Fig 2-39**. This is a very useful tool for all kinds of things.

Look down the line items in the box. From here you can change the layer, the color, the weight of the line, the angle of lines can be adjusted, most qualities of an object can be edited here. This can be used for recalling the properties of hatches (if you forget the settings) and editing them. Play around with the Properties dialog box and see what it can do for you.

One of the most useful functions of the **Properties** box is to edit dimensions and their text.

Make sure you see the properties box for the dimension—it is labeled at the top. It is easy to click on the wrong object after you open the properties box. You can leave the properties box open and click on different objects. Use the ESC to unselect an object before selecting another object.

Use the **slide bar** on the **left** of the **Properties box** to **scroll down** until the **Text** section is fully displayed. Click in the empty box next to **Text override** (you may need to widen the Properties box to read the options: place the cursor on the right edge of the box until it changes shape and pull it out/do this at the bottom of the box to make it longer). **Click** in the Text Override box a second time to get the cursor line pulsating. Now type: **28' 3"** (**here you must enter** the " for inches) <e>. It should change the dimension to read just that.

 While you are here, try a few other things. At the **Text position vert**, click in that box where it says "Centered". Change the settings from centered to "Above". These settings can be very useful when you have trouble placing the dimension text in tight spots and need to be creative about the placement of text. **ESC** and **Close** the Properties box.

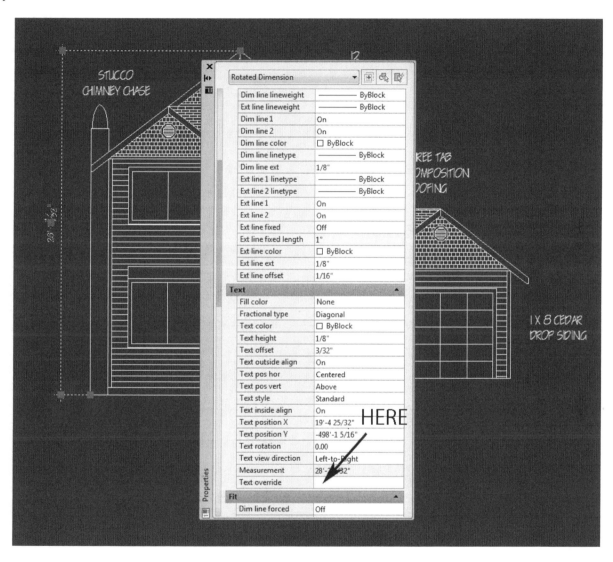

Fig 2-39

Set the **0 Layer** current and draw the door details. Use **4" offset** for the styles and rails (these are the lines in the door). Use **Offset**, **Extend** and **Trim** to get the lines you see in Fig 2-38. You are done with this view!

The Rest of the Stories (Elevations)

.

If you wish to draw the other three elevations use the drawings in Appendix IV. You can draw the second story and use it for reference or you can simply measure the windows and place them by measurements as we did in this chapter.

There you go. You are about half way through this course. Even though you are only a third of the way through the pages, the process accelerates as you go along.

Chapter 3—Plot the Elevations

3.1 Prepare the Elevations Page

With what you have learned so far you can draw a full set of house plans. You should be able to draw just about anything. There are still a number of procedures and drawing tools that are useful and make drawing faster and easier, but the basics that you have learned so far are enough to produce most drawings.

Now you need to know how to print, email and plot your plans. This chapter is all about printing, plotting and sending PDF copies of your drawings. Plotting and printing is one of the most complex parts of AutoCAD. Fortunately you will not need to know everything about this subject—just enough to do your job.

In this chapter we will prepare the Elevation page of the drawings. It is the simplest of the pages because it depicts four views that are basically the same size and shape and the entire page is plotted at ¼" = 1' scale (commonly called **quarter inch scale or quarter scale**).

First we are going to produce a 36" x 24" page. This is the most common size for use in the construction industry. In addition to the 36 x 24 pages we will set up for 11 x 8.5 printing. This is a handy size for mailing and carrying to meetings. It is also a common size for mechanical drawings and engineering details. Finally we will produce PDF files of the plans that can be attached to emails.

A number of the methods demonstrated in this book illustrate unique ways of producing drawings (my own personal techniques). The production of the 36 x 24 sheets, as demonstrated here, falls into that category. It describes a specific technique for producing printed/plotted drawings that is fast and simple. You can use this method for now and then design your own style and procedure later.

Fig 3-1

Look at Fig 3-1. It represents a completed page of the Elevation plan (Page 2 of the plan set) to be plotted on 36 x 24 inch paper. It includes the title block with a border around the edge of the sheet and the four elevation views with titles. Here we will prepare and plot just the views.

After we plot this page you will be able to use a measuring device (a measuring tape, a ruler or a scale) and each ¼" measured on the page will equal 1 foot of the actual building.

Let's create a rectangle of the appropriate sized area on our AutoCAD workspace. Off to one side in your workspace draw a **rectangle 128' x 92'**. Use the **Construction layer** for this rectangle. Now copy the four different elevations into this rectangle as shown in **Fig 3-2**.

For those of you have not drawn all four elevations, copy the front elevation that you drew to all four locations, just to block out the spaces (the important information here is the layout of the page not the completed elevation views). See Fig 3-17 to see what this looks like.

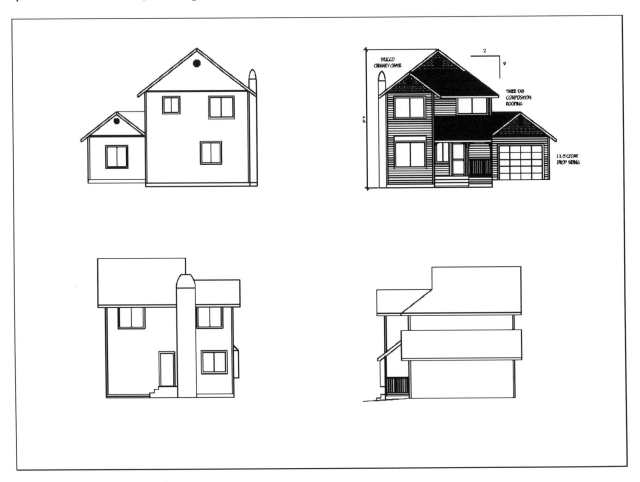

Fig 3-2

This area represents the part of the 36 x 24 paper that is inside the borders—the paper size minus a small border area and the title block. We will draw the border and title block later.

The page will look better if the four elevation views are lined up. So draw a line at the bottom of the two lower views and set your drawings so that they are **in line with each other**. Do not worry about exact placement. You can set them by eye. The idea is that the page should look balanced and neat.

Draw another line and **align** the two top views. See **Fig 3-3**.

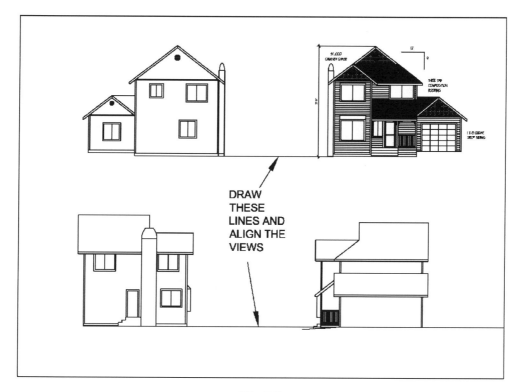

DRAW
THESE
LINES AND
ALIGN THE
VIEWS

Fig 3-3

Now we need to draw the view titles (see Fig 3-1). **Fig 3-4** shows the **lines** and **layout**.

THESE LINES ARE 50' LONG

THERE ARE
THREE LINES

THIS IS WHAT IT LOOKS LIKE WITH THE TEXT:

SOUTH ELEVATION

SCALE 1/4" = 1'

Fig 3-4

Beneath the upper right elevation, draw a line **50 feet** long. **Offset** it by **18"** (below) and again by **1.5"** as shown in **Fig 3-4**. Use the **Text layer**.

In the **Object Snap** settings turn on the **Insertion** osnap. This creates a base point for text.

In open space off to the side open an **MText** box (type **mt <e>**). Set the **font style** to **City Blue**. Set the **text height to 18"** and use **Bold** print. **Type** the words: SOUTH ELEVATION (use two spaces between the words—titles look better with two spaces between words). Use **Middle/Center** for the **justification** (use the justification button on the Paragraph palette that opens when you open a Mtext box or see Appendix I—Text). This means centered both horizontally and vertically.

Draw a **diagonal line** as shown in **Fig 3-6**.

Highlight the **text** (SOUTH ELEVATION), **grab** it by the **center** blue **grip** box, and **move** it to the **midpoint** of this **diagonal line** as in **Fig 3-6**. **Erase** the diagonal line.

This is an alternate method of **moving text**: type it, click on the OK in the text formatting bar or Close Text Editor on the ribbon. Highlight the text by clicking on it or select it with a selection window, then move it by the center blue grip. It is a good way to **center text between two lines**.

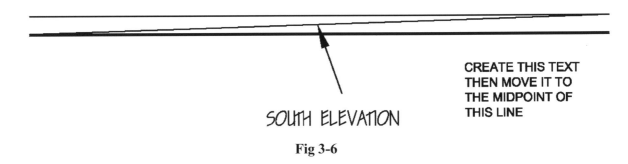

CREATE THIS TEXT
THEN MOVE IT TO
THE MIDPOINT OF
THIS LINE

SOUTH ELEVATION

Fig 3-6

Now open the **Mtext** box again and set the text height to **6"** (I always use bold for light weight font texts like City Blueprint). **Type: SCALE ¼" = 1'**. Use a space both sides of the equal sign. **Copy** this to the approximate space shown in **Fig 3-4 and Fig 3-7**. Set it by eye for now.

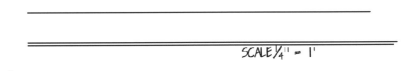

SCALE ¼" = 1'

Fig 3-7

Copy this title to the other **three locations** shown in **Fig 3-1**. Set them by eye or you can create temporary construction lines as you choose. **Highlight** and **edit** the **text** to read the different compass directions (**NORTH, EAST**, and **WEST**) shown in **Fig 3-1**.

To give our view titles a little flair we may want to make the lines uneven as you see them in Fig 3-7. Highlight the lines and with the Ortho turned on, use the blue grip boxes to stretch them out or shrink them a bit. This is strictly per eye, there is no formula (and not all drafters do this). You will need to turn off the Osnap or the line will want to keep snapping back to the original end point.

3.2 Page Set up

Now we are ready to plot.

At the bottom of the workspace you will see the **Model** and **Layout** tabs (**1** in **Fig 3-8**).

> If the **Layout tab**(s) **do not display** on your screen then type: Options/ then Display/ and check the box that says: Display Layout and Model tabs.

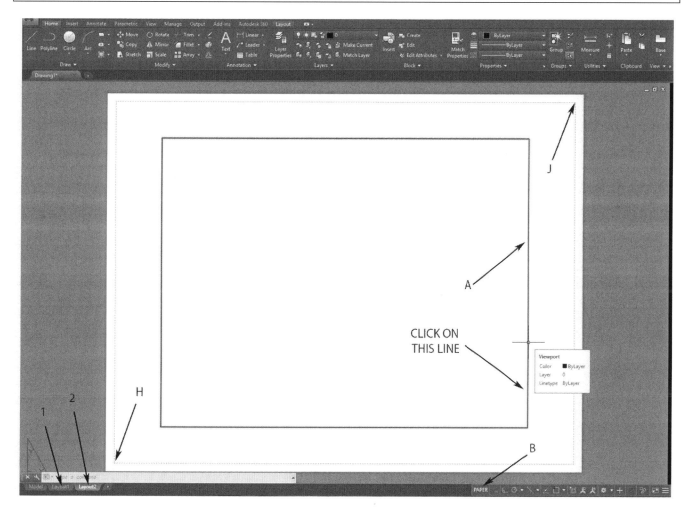

Fig 3-8

Right click on the first **Layout** tab (1) select: **New Layout**. A new Layout tab will appear to the right (**2**).

Click on this **new tab** (You may have more tabs than shown in Fig 3-8, just click on the one furthest to the right). This will bring up a white section. This can vary a lot in how it appears, but it is supposed to represent a piece of white paper. **Click** on the tab at **B** in **Fig 3-8** and you will see that it switches between **Model** and **Paper**. **Set** it to **Paper**. Type **z** <e> then **a** <e> (zoom all) to see the entire sheet of paper.

There will be an inner **rectangle** as at **A** in **Fig 3-8**. **Click** on rectangle **A**.

You may have to highlight rectangle A before you can select it (depending on your system settings). It can be difficult to highlight so move your cursor slowly back and forth across it until the line becomes bold (this means it is highlighted) and click. When it is selected (it will show **blue grip boxes** at the four corners when it is selected) **erase** it (remember you can use the **delete** on your computer keyboard to erase).

Now back at the **Layout** tab (your new layout tab), **right click,** and select **Page Setup Manager**… from the menu that appears. You can also type Pagesetup in the command line.

A **Page Setup Manager** box will open. Select **New**. When the **New Page Setup** box opens type **36x24** for the **new name**, **click** on the **OK**. The box shown in **Fig 3-9 will open**.

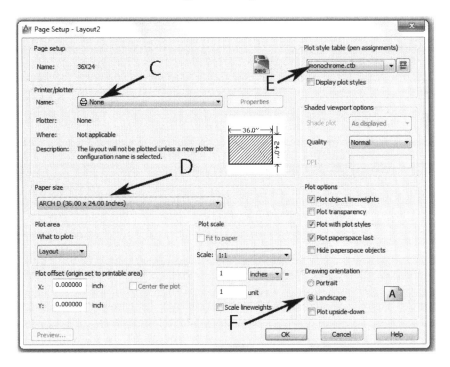

Fig 3-9

Set it as shown in **Fig 3-9**. At **C** set it to **none**. At **D** set it as shown. At **E** set it to **monochrom**.ctb. Set **F** to **Landscape**. Click on **OK**. **Close** the **Page Setup Manager** dialog box.

In the **Page Setup** manager **click** on the **Set Current** button.

Right click again on the **new Layout tab,** and from the **menu**, select **Rename**. The name in the tab will highlight blue. Type: **36x24 <e>**. This new name will appear in the layout tab.

Create a **new Layer** in the **Layer Properties Manager**. Name it **viewport** and make it **black**. At the **Printer icon** as **shown** in **Fig 3-9A**, turn **off** the **printer** (click on it). Now this layer will not print. Set this **layer current**.

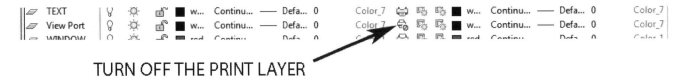

TURN OFF THE PRINT LAYER

Fig 3-9A

Select the **Layout** ribbon and click on the **Rectangular** button (it is co-located with the polygon and object button—Fig 3-10) on the Layout Viewports palette (this only appears when a Layout tab is selected). Now click on point **H** in **Fig 3-8** then click on point **J**. It may take a few moments or even a minute to **regenerate** the **Model**. Then a **viewport will open**. This is a view through the paper into the model space behind.

When you open a viewport, it is as if the paper has become transparent and you are holding it up to the model workspace screen on your computer: you are looking through the paper at model space.

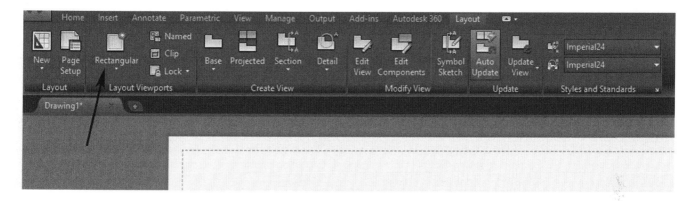

Fig 3-10

Double click in the center of this paper space and the Model/Paper button at the bottom will switch to **Model** (Or click on the Paper/Model button at the bottom of the screen so that Model is displayed—B in Fig 3-8).

Type **z <e>**. then **a<e>** (that is Zoom All). You should now see your entire workspace (everything on your model space screen—called the work space).

Find the elevations as in Fig 3-11. We want to center them in the middle of our paper viewport. Try using the Zoom window (the zoom window button or type **z <e> w <e>**). Then **open** a **selection window around** the **four elevations**.

Use the center mouse wheel to move the four elevations around and place them in the approximate center of the paper as in **Fig 3-11**.

There is the possibility of confusion between Model space and Paper space as selected by the Model tab and the Layout tab and the Model/Paper space button. You can see these in Fig 1-1. Fig 3-8 shows the Layout tabs next to the Model tab designated 1 and 2 and the Paper/Model space button designated as B.

The tabs take you to Model space or Paper space. The Paper/Model button sets the Layout to either the paper or the model space behind (within) the paper. When it is set to Paper this allows you to open a viewport, adjust the settings for the viewport, set the size, lock the viewport, and scroll in and out on the paper. The Model setting opens model space inside the viewport. Now when you scroll in and out you zoom in and out in model space. This allows you to select what you want centered in the viewport and set it to the desired plotting scale.

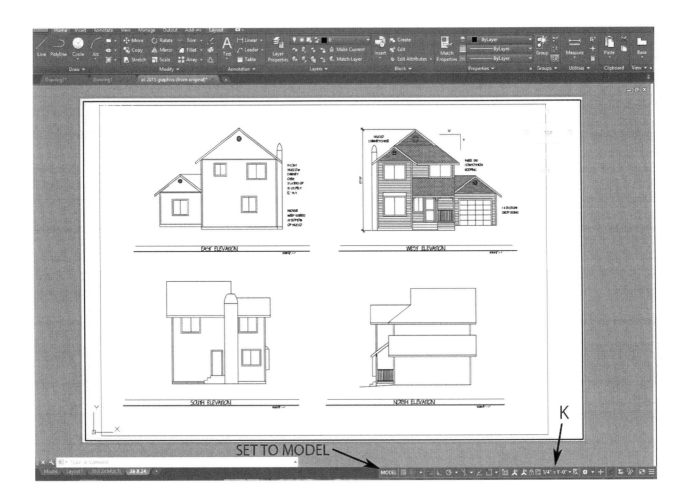

Fig 3-11

Down at the bottom right of the computer screen click on the down arrow in the button shown at **K** in **Fig 3-11** and **Fig 3-12**. This is the **Viewport scale**. A list of scales will appear in a box as shown in **Fig 3-12**.

Find the **1/4" = 1' scale** (at **L** in Fig 3-12) and **click** on it (You may need to scroll down by using the scroll bar to the right of this window (it is thin and hard to see so run your cursor over the right edge until it highlights). Your drawing will adjust to fill the page. It is now ¼" scale (short for ¼" = 1'scale). Center your four elevations drawing in the viewport by grabbing it with the mouse center button and moving it where you want it. Don't worry too much about exact placement just yet.

After you position the drawing in the viewport set the scale again as it can change a tiny bit while you are panning with the mouse wheel. This is important when the scale must be exact.

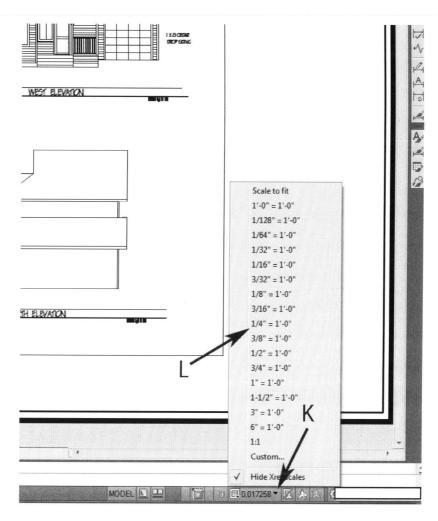

Fig 3-12

This page is ready to plot.

You can **lock** the scale (1/4" = 1') in place by setting the space to **Paper** (use the button at the bottom of the screen: B in Fig 3-8). Select the viewport by clicking on the line of the viewport, when it highlights with the blue grip boxes, right click. Where it says **Display locked** click on the down arrow next to the No and change it to Yes.

Note: the **broken lines** shown in Fig 3-8 are **not** the **viewport**. They are the margin lines—the limits that the printer will print. Printers usually have a small space around the edge of the paper where they will not print.

The lines of the viewport and the paper space can become altered, sometimes spontaneously. See Appendix I—Viewport if this happens and you wish to change it back.

If you decide to lock the viewport, remember that it is locked when you want to change the view in the future. You must **unlock** it before you can **make** any **changes**.

Okay so we are ready to plot, but we need to tell AutoCAD what printer we are going to use.

We must set up a plotter.

3.3 Plotter Setup for 36 x 24

Click on the **Output** ribbon tab. Select **Plotter Manager**. The box shown in **Fig 3-13** will open (you can type plottermanager). Select the **Add-A-Plotter Wizard** by double clicking on it (as shown in Fig 3-13). If double clicking does not open it then highlight it, right click and select Open. Now a series of windows will open that have three buttons at the bottom. It is the **Next button** that we are most interested in. The first box will be titled "**Introduction Page**". Click **Next**. The "**Begin**" page will open. Select the **My Computer radio button**. Click **Next**.

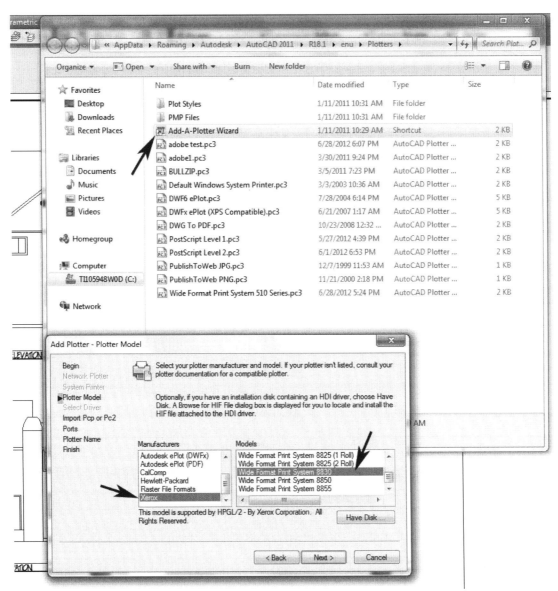

Fig 3-13

This is the "**Plotter Model**" page. You will need to select a **Manufacturer** and **model** of a **Plotter**. This is the plotting machine you will use to print out the 36 x 24 inch copies. Every sizable town has a blue print office where you can have your plans printed (also copy shops, like Kinkos, will often print this size). You will need to call and find out what kind of copier/plotter they are using. They will tell you the model and you can **enter** that **information** by selecting it from the list of Manufacturers and Models shown in Fig 3-13.

My local blue print office uses a **Xerox 8830 Wide Format** print system plotter. That is what I have selected in **Fig 3-13**.

If you do not know the name of the local plotter (the model used locally), then you can use the settings in this book for now and set up another plotter later (you can set up as many plotters and copiers as you want).

Click **Next**. This is the "**Import Pcp or Pc2**" page. We don't need to deal with this for now. Click **Next**.

This is the "Ports" page. Click on **Plot to File** at the top center. This is going to create a plot file on your computer that you can send over the internet as an email attachment, or copy the file onto a disc (or flash drive) and carry it to the office where the plotter/copier is located.

It is easy to miss this setting the first few times you set up a plotter and it can drive you a bit nuts trying to figure out why your plotting is not producing a file. So remember to check this step if you have a problem.

The next page is the "**Plotter Name**". The model of the printer that you selected should appear here or you can add it. Click **Next**.

Click **Finish**.

You will see that the **printer/plotter** that you set up **is now listed** in the **Plotter manager** box. **Close** this box.

Back at the work space **right click** on the **36x24 layout tab** at the bottom of the screen (**2 in Fig 3-8**).

Click on **Plot**. A **Plot window will open**. You should have everything set from Fig 3-9 except the selection of the printer. To do this, **select the printer** that you just set up in the window shown at **C** in **Fig 3-9**. Where it says **Name**, you can name the page Xerox or the name of your chosen plotter. Check the other settings as in Fig 3-9.

Check out the little **window expansion arrow** all the way down in the lower right corner. This collapses and expands the window . Which, again, raises the question: why half a window?

At the bottom where it says **Apply to Layout**—**click**. Then **click** on the **preview button** to see what the page will look like when plotted. **Close** the **preview** (x at the top of the screen) and click **OK**.

A box will open that allows you to **name the plot file**. **Name it: paradise3.PLT** (Paradise is the street name of our fictional project and this is the third page of the plans) and select a destination. Save it on the **desktop** for now if you don't have a preference.

Eventually you will want to create a document folder for all of your AutoCAD drawings and PLT files. You can do this now if you want and store everything there. Go to Documents on your computer and create a new folder. Name it AutoCAD or whatever.

Minimize AutoCAD and **look at the desktop** (or in your new folder); you should **see** your **PLT file** there. If not then you will need to go back through the steps again and see if you missed anything. See Appendix IV—Plotting for further assistance.

Now you can copy this PLT file on to a **disc** and take it to the local office where they have the printer and they will print it out for you. You can also attach it to an **email** and send it to the printer.

Now we will set up another layout, for printing on your copier/printer at home or in the office.

3.4 Plotter Setup for 11 x 8.5

We will essentially follow the same steps as the process in **3.3 Plotter Set up for 36 x 24.** Review that section if you need to refresh your memory.

In order to plot to your **home** or **office printer** you may need to have the **driver** for the printer/copier **installed** on your computer. If the driver is not installed it may not show up in the list of plotters when you get to that step. In that case you will need to install the driver. Your printer/copier most likely came with a disc that contains the driver. You can insert the disc and follow the instructions. **If you do not have the driver disc then go online** to the website of the manufacturer of your copier/printer and they will have the driver online that you can download. Before you do that, go through the steps that follow and see if your copier printer shows up in the list of plotters already listed.

Connect you computer to your printer/copier as you would normally to print off the computer.

Create a new **Layout tab** by **right clicking** on the **36x24** Layout tab (**2** in **Fig 3-8**). This will create a new layout tab to the right.

Click on the newly created **Layout** tab. It may take a minute to load.

Once the new layout is added, **right click** on the tab and select the **Page Setup Manager** (just as before). Click **New**. **Name** it **11x8.5**. In the **Page Set-up** box set everything as in **Fig 3-14**. In the **Printer/plotter** window scroll down until you see your printer/copier and select it. Set the **paper size** to **Letter** (most important). Set the **Plot Style Table** (pen assignments) to **monochrome.ctb**. Then select the **Landscape** setting at the bottom right. **OK**.

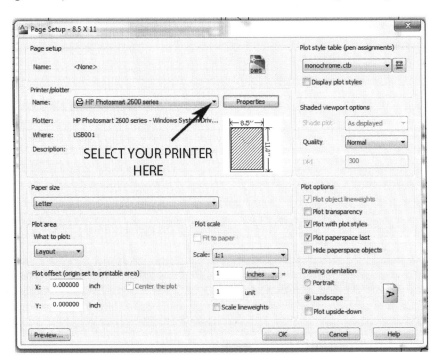

Fig 3-14

Right click on the new layout tab and **name** it **11x8.5**. A new 11 x 8.5 inch paper space "piece of paper" will replace the 36 x 24. It will have a viewport in the middle (not the dashed lines—those represent the margins for the selected printer).

As before, **erase** the **viewport** (set the **space** to **Paper** and move the cursor slowly over one of the viewport lines until it highlights then select it and erase).

Create a **new single viewport** that covers the entire page (or between the dashed lines if they are showing). This is shown at H and J in Fig 3-8.

Select **Model** space from the Model/Paper button at the bottom of the screen (B in Fig 3-8). Select the east view elevation drawing by using the mouse wheel to move it. Place this in the center of the viewport and **set the scale to ¼" = 1'**.

Move the elevation around to see (approximately) as in **Fig 3-15**. Some of the text is off the page but that is okay for now (you can reposition the text and place it on the page).

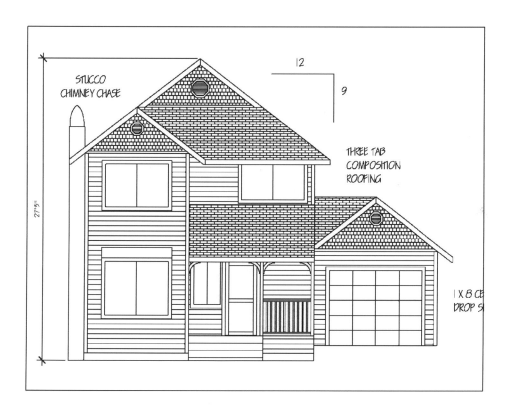

Fig 3-15

Right click the **11x8.5 tab** again and go to **Page Setup Manager. Highlight the 11x8.5** and click **Modify. Check** the **settings**. They should look like Fig 3-14. If they have changed then reset them. Click **OK**. This layout is ready to print out on your copier.

Close the **Page Setup Manager. Right click** on the **11x8.5 tab**. Select **Plot** and **OK**. You can look at the Preview before you print (close it after the preview then click OK).

Now you can see why the house was designed to the size that it is—each view fits on an 8.5 x 11 piece of paper when printed at ¼" = 1' scale. The same is true with the floor plan and the details.

Try a different scale. In paper space select Model from the Model/Paper (B in Fig 3-8) button space and this time select the 3/32 = 1' scale. You will see Fig 3-16 (more or less). Set the scale back to ¼" for printing of the single elevation.

Fig 3-16

3.5 Plot a PDF

Now we will create a **PDF** file that you can attach to an email or send in a disc to someone through the mail.

In order to create a PDF that is larger than letter size you must have a **PDF creating program installed on your computer** that creates the size that you want or use the DWG to PDF.pc3 setting in the Printer/Plotter menu shown in Fig 3-14. There are a number of free PDF creating software programs available on the internet. If you do not see the DWG to PDF.pc3 option in the Printer/Plotter selection list, add it by following the instructions at the end of this chapter.

Basically you will follow the same steps as in Section 3.4. The only difference is that you will select the **PDF creator** in the **Plotter/printer** window as in **Fig 3-14** (you do not have to use the Add-A-Plotter Wizard). You do not need to name this Layout at the top. When you click **OK** you will see the **"Save PDF File As"** screen; **name** the file and send the PDF file to the desktop (or your new folder).

You can now open the PDF file (if you can't then you will need to download Acrobat Reader from the internet).

You can send this as an attachment to an email.

That is it for this chapter. The AutoCAD in 20 Hours deals with the printing and plotting process in more detail.

Fig 3-17 shows what the page looks like if you have not drawn all four elevations. The front elevation is used in all four locations as a place marker; these can be replaced with the real elevations if they are drawn.

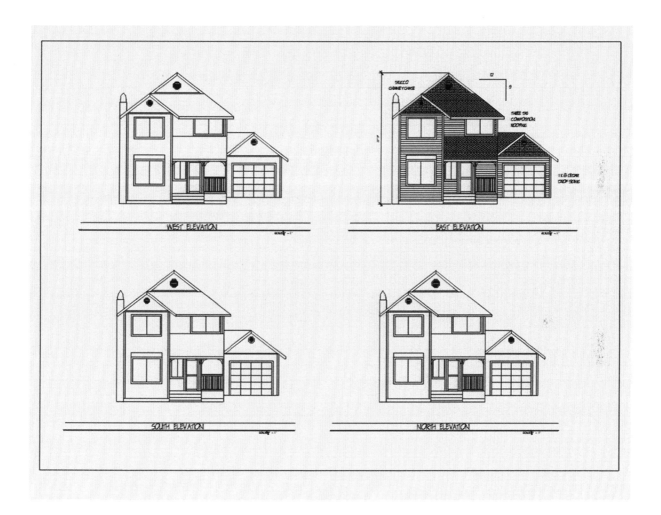

Fig 3-17

Add the DWG to PDF.pc3 Plotter.

1. Open the Add a Plotter Wizard (see Plotter Setup page 150).
2. Select Autodesk ePlot (PDF).
3. Click Next and use the default settings, continue until Finish.

You should now see this selection in the Printer/Plotter list.

Appendix I   General Information

General help under alphabetic categories

Arc

If you turn on the Dynamic Input function (located with the Ortho and Osnap buttons at the bottom of the screen) you can see the length and angle of the arc that you are creating using the 3-Point. You can get it close to what you want, and then customize the arc using the properties palette or one of the other Arc tools. Which too depends on what parameters are important. Radius is a common definition used. The Start,End,Radius Arc tool is good for this. Look at the list and try out the different options to see which tool is best for each parameter.

Cursor settings

You can customize the settings for your cursor and selection boxes. Type **options** to open the **Options** dialog box. Click on the **Drafting** tab. This will open a dialog box where you can change the size of your cursor and Osnap icon size.

Chamfer and Fillet

Both chamfer and fillet can be set by reading the prompts and making selections as you go through the set up process. Watch for the **Multiple** option and type m. This will allow you to fillet or chamfer a series of corners without having to go through the whole process each time.

Command Line

If you lose the command line press Ctrl 9. If this doesn't work try typing: commandline. The command line can be expanded or reduced by grabbing the border with the cursor (it will turn into a little H grip) and sliding it up or down. It can be placed in different places on the screen by using the grip in the upper left corner.

Dashed Lines

Model Space Problems: if your dashed lines do not show as dashed lines in model space. Check your settings for ltscale, msltscale, celtscale.

Ltscale sets the scale for all lines in the drawing. Type ltscale to set the value. Try some experimental lines using different linetypes (set them as different layers). Then try different scales and see what you get.

Celtscale sets the linetype value for the next object drawn (and everything after that until you reset it) without changing the overall scale that is set with the ltscale setting. The properties palette can also be used for this.

Msltscale sets the linetype to annotative. A value of 1 makes the linetypes annotative, 0 is non-annotative.

Properites palette can be used to change the line characteristics for individual or groups of lines.

Paper Space Problems: Dashed lines can be a bit difficult at times. A common problem is when they do not show up as dashed lines in the **paperspace** viewport or when plotted/printed. If you have this problem the first thing to do is to reset your **paperspace linetype** scale. Type: **psltscale** and set the value to **0**. Then **regen** the drawing and they should appear. To regen type **Regenall**. Wait a bit, it can take some time.

You can easily change the scale of your dashed or broken lines by using the **Properties** palate. Click on a line to select it then right click on choose the **Properties** option. Change the line type scale.

Set up linestyles in the Layer Properties Manager (Appendix II). When you click on the linetype (where it says Continu…) you bring up the **Select Linetype** window. Click on **Load** and the **Load or Reload Linetypes** window will open. The size of the dashes that will appear on your drawing is determined by which of these lines you select and then by the linetype scale for the entire drawing that is set by typing **ltscale** and setting a value. You will need to play around with this a bit to find the setting that you want.

There are only five standard dashed lines listed, but you can rescale any of these using the **Properties palette** in the model workspace. Use the **match properties** to change all of the lines that you want to be the same scale.

Design Center

The design center can be difficult to navigate. Follow the directions in Chapter 1, Section 1.19 for an explanation of how to find the preset graphics.

In this book we only use the most basic function of the design center. That is to import graphics. You can find a lot more graphics by going online.

Many companies that sell construction products also have cad graphics of their products that you can import into your drawings. As an example go online and search for kohler cad drawings. There you will find lists of cad drawings of their plumbing products that can be imported into your drawings. You can copy and paste these drawings. Select the graphic with a selection window, then use Ctrl+C, go to your drawing and place it with Ctrl+V.

Dimensions

Dimension styles are set in the **Dimension Styles Manager** dialog box. You can access it by clicking on the Dimension Style manager button in the Annotation palette or type: **dimstyle**. You start out with a Standard and an Annotative Style preset.

To **create** a **new style**: click on one of these two (depending on if you want annotative or not) and then the "**New**" button. This is all detailed in Chapter 1 Section 1.23.

Whether you use the Annotative feature or set your dimension style manually, you will need to know what scale you intend to plot to (or print out). Determine this before you create dimensions or text on your drawing. The ratio of that scale is then entered into the **Use Overall Scale of** window under the **Fit** tab when you are using a non-**annotative dimstyle**.

If an object is **scaled in model space** then the **inverse** of that **scale** must be **entered** into the **Scale factor** window under the **Primary Units** tab.

The other settings in Dimstyle are easy to understand and the display window shows you the results of changing the settings.

Angular dimensions (not 90 degree vertical or horizontal) are added with the **Aligned** dimension tool on the Annotation palette (co-located with the Linear button).

Electrical Symbols

Fig A-1 shows the progression of the electrical symbol for a light. Draw a 6" circle, offset it to the outside by 1.5". Next draw the lines by using the Quadrant Osnap. Erase the outer circle and trim to see the light symbol.

Fig A-1

Fig A-2 shows the progression of the outlet drawing. Start with a 6" circle. Draw a 9" line and place its midpoint on the center of the circle using the Center Osnap. Offset this line to each side by 1". Erase the middle line and draw a line between the two end points of the two outside lines. Offset this line by 1". Now copy this symbol (but not the short horizontal line). Use the midpoint of the short horizontal line as your base point for copying. Remember that when you copy or move an object the base point (the point you will use to snap to an Osnap icon) doesn't need to be a part of the object you copy. You can use any point on the workspace as your base point.

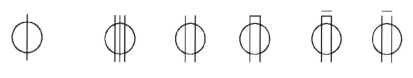

Fig A-2

Fig A-3 shows the electrical symbols enlarged.

Fig A-3

Extend

Extend is one of the commands that can be difficult. It doesn't always work the first time. Often it is necessary to **double click** on the command button in order for the system to recognize the command. See **Trim and Extend** later in this appendix for a discussion of Extend.

First Line

UCS sometimes interferes with the identity of the first line. To turn it off click on the View tab then on the UCS icon to the far left.

The UCS can be placed anywhere on the workspace. Also read Line in this appendix, if you still have problems with the Line command.

Fraction stacking.

Fractions can be typed in various styles. Type the fraction then **highlight it** with the cursor. **Right click** on the highlighted text and choose **Stack or Unstack**. There is also a button on the Text Editor ribbon and the Text Formatting bar.

Glitches

AutoCad has a lot of glitches in the system. I have experienced numerous glitches with several different editions (years) and different computers. This is an impossible subject to cover here because there are so many variables, but if strange things happen, you can look in the different headings in this appendix to see if a specific glitch is covered.

One pesky glitch is that the system will start up and tell you that your settings were not saved. Then it will open, and many of your settings will be gone. You can look for a back up file, these are **.bak** files. You may be able to open a bak file to restore and save your settings. Look for the bak files in your computer files. You may not find them by clicking on Open in your AutoCad program.

If you cannot find the bak file, you will have to recreate your settings: layers, dimension and text styles. If you have a set up file you can copy and paste your drawing into a copy of that to restore your settings. Type units and make sure the system has not changed unit settings.

It seems as though many of the system settings can change on their own. Unfortunately this is one area that cannot be covered because there are too many different forms that this can take. Usually this means resetting the settings one by one. Many of the settings are found in the Options window under the Tool tab at the top of the screen.

If you are trying to do something in this book, and it just doesn't seem to work, you may need to consider that certain settings have been altered. Try saving your file, exiting AutoCad and restarting your computer. Then restart AutoCad and see if that fixes the system. Check any settings that may be associated with the function that is not working.

There is a system reset (reset to defaults). This is found on your computer. Go to start (often just an icon in the lower left corner of your screen), go to All Programs, find AutoDesk and find: **Reset Settings to Default**. This will set everything back to the way it came out of the box. This can resolve some of the stranger system errors that occur from time to time.

Gradient

Hatch and Gradient function the same basic way. See Chapter 2, Section 2.10 for the steps involved with Hatch/Gradient.

Hatch is a pattern and Gradient is a color fill (or two colors). The color can be a gradient between two colors or a gradient from light to dark. This is set with the **one** or **two color** setting. Use Solid to get a single color fill.

The best way to understand Gradient is to create a rectangle of say 10 ft x 10 ft and then try the different settings. First try one color and see what you get. Then try two colors and see what you get.

The biggest problem with Hatch and Gradient is selecting the **Pick points**. Quite often the system fails to recognize the enclosed space that you select. The reason for this is usually that there are micro openings in the corners. The Hatch/Gradient needs a completely enclosed space in order to function. Otherwise it would spill out and fill up the entire workspace (it doesn't do this—you get an error window).

AutoCAD will create gaps in the corners that were previously closed. This can be very difficult to find because they can be microscopic. The tolerances for AutoCad are extremely minute. See Hatch in this appendix for more on this.

Hatch

Sometimes Hatch locks up and the system becomes **unresponsive**. If this happens use the **Esc** key and try again. Give it a minute (or two) to respond. You may need to do this several times.

The biggest problem with hatch is that it requires that the space to be filled with the hatch or gradient must be completely enclosed—there can be **no gaps** between the enclosing lines. Sometimes you think an area is completely enclosed by lines but it is, in fact, not.

AutoCAD operates to very minute tolerances and you can have a **microscopic gap** where two lines meet. Use the extend tool to make sure the corners are all enclosed if you find that Hatch or Gradient cannot define the space to be filled.

Sometimes **gaps will open after you have them closed**. This is a glitch in the system and it can really throw you for a loop. If the system says it cannot define the space then you must go back to all the corners and make sure they are closed. Even the extend feature will not sometimes close up entirely. So if you really cannot seem to get the system to define the enclosed space you may try drawing the lines beyond the point where they intersect and then trim them back—they won't trim unless they are crossing (and that means closed). You can also try adding more lines and subdivide the area into smaller sections. This will help isolate the problem area.

Another irritating problem with hatch and gradient is that sometimes AutoCAD will not select the hatch or the gradient for editing (or erasing). You can try to zoom in and select a large area with the green selection window. Sometimes you just have to keep trying different zoomed parts of the Hatch until you can highlight it.

If you find that the program simply won't recognize the hatch for selection, you can turn off the other layers around the hatch. Then try to select the entire hatch with a selection window. If all else fails you can turn off all the other layers and erase the hatch or gradient, and replace it.

Keyboard

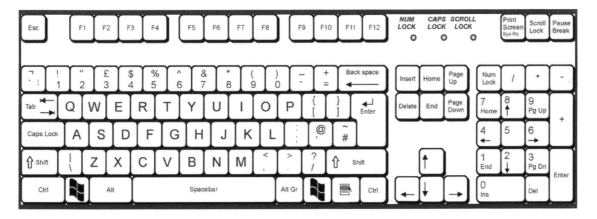

Fig A-4

The F keys are the top row. F3 toggles **Osnap** and F8 toggles **Ortho**.

Enter in this book means hit the enter button on the keyboard (also: **<ent>** or just **<e>**).

For some operations you must hold down the **Control** key while you press another key at the same time. Here the control key can be seen in the lower left hand corner marked **Ctrl**.

Cap locks are on the left side.

Layers

Make certain to turn off the plot setting for layers that you do not want plotted/printed before you plot. This will usually mean the Viewport Layer, but also any construction lines or temporary line layers. Do this in the Layer properties Manager (Appendix II). There is a column with a little printer. Click on it and it will show a red line accross the printer icon.

Layers are set and controlled in the **Layer Properties Manager**. Here you can create a new layer with a dedicated line type. See Chapter 1 Section 1.18 (Fig 1-37) for details on setting up Layers.

Layer Control sets the current layer and allows you to change the layer of an object (select the object then click on the layer in the Layer Control you want to change it to). Here you can also turn specific layers off or on (the little light bulb symbol), freeze or thaw layers, and lock the layers so they can't be altered.

Leaders
This book only deals with **Qleaders**.

Leaders have to be a **certain length before the arrowhead shows**. This is about 3 times longer than the arrowhead.

The settings for leaders are found in two different places.

The **size** of leaders is set with the **Dimension Style Manager**. If you want to change the size of the leader you must change the current dimension style. Set the dimension style for the scale you will be plotting before you draw the leader.

These plans are plotted at ¼" scale. For these pages you would set the quarter dimension style which is set up to print at the scale of ¼" = 1'.

The **arrowhead size** and some other aspects of the leader are set in the **Symbols and Arrow** tab. Click on the **Dimension Style Manager** button on the Annotation palette or type **dimstyle <e>**. Chose a style and click on the Modify button. There you will see the Symbols and Arrows tab.

Some of the **leader settings** are **located** in **another location**. Type **qleader**. Read the prompts in the command line. When it reads: specify first point, or [Settings] <Settings>: **type s** and hit the **enter** key. (This is the way a lot of commands work: all you need to do is type the first letter of a word that is listed in the prompts). When you do this, a **Leader Settings** box opens. There you can set your annotation. For this book you set it to **None**. Then under the leader line and arrow you can set the line to either straight lines or spline (curved lines). Set the number of points that determine the shape of the spline (**no limits** for this book), Angle restraints (**Any angle** for this book), and the shape of the leader arrowhead. **Okay.**

Annotative leaders will be set with the Dimension Style manager. They will self adjust to the scale set in the Annotation Scale window at the bottom of the Model workspace screen.

Line
If you are trying to draw the first line of a drawing and it just won't draw a line, it may be that the **units** are **not set correctly**. AutoCAD has a glitch in the system whereby it does not always set the system units when you set them in the page setup. Type: **units.** Then make certain that your settings are correct (for this book you want **Architectural** and **inches** as the insertion scale).

Lines, like most objects display **grip boxes** when you select the line as shown in Fig A-5.

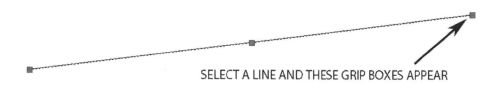

SELECT A LINE AND THESE GRIP BOXES APPEAR

Fig A-5

You can turn these on by clicking on the line (selecting it). Blue grip boxes will appear. If you click on one of the blue grip boxes it will turn red. If you do this to the end of the line you can stretch the line. You can pull it out a ways and enter in a number for the extension that you desire. You can also rotate it from the end box. If you grip it in the middle it will move the entire line.

This can be a good way to trim and extend lines when those functions are not responding properly.

There are a number of ways to draw lines. **Angled lines** can be draw with a **written description** in the command window. Click **line** then, then specify the first point (start of the line), then enter the description of where the line goes from that first point. You enter the **length** first and then the **angle**. The format is as follows for a 10'6" line that is at an angle of 45 degrees: type **@10'6<45** (enter).

Most often it is easiest to start a **right angle** line by specifying a first (starting) point, pull a ways in the direction you wish to draw the line (with the **Ortho** on) and then type the length.

If you are drawing a lot of lines with a certain degree you can use polar tracking and set the accuracy to include the angle you will draw. Set this by right clicking on the **Polar Tracking**. See Polar Tracking in this Appendix.

Lines can also be drawn using coordinates. These reference the UCS origin point. You can set a UCS origin point anywhere in the drawing and then type line coordinates. Enter the horizontal measurement first, then the vertical. Both points on the line (the start and end) will have two coordinates. This is not especially helpful, but is good to keep in mind for certain applications.

Linetypes
See Dashed Lines

Mirror
Mirror is a simple tool to use. The only complicated part of it is that the mirror line between the two (right and left) views of the object is not a line that you draw with the line tool. It is a line that you create in the process of the Mirror command. Try this to see what this means. Use the mirror tool. Turn the ortho on. Select an object to mirror. Read the prompts. When the prompt says: Specify first point of mirror line, click on the empty space next to and above your object (that you want to mirror). Then pull the line that appears down. This is the mirror line. So, as you can see, you do not need to draw a line with the line tool.

The other thing about mirror is that you almost certainly want to use the **ortho** when creating a **mirror line**. If you experiment with this command for a few minutes you will see how it works.

Mouse settings

The mouse can be set to function in various ways. Of course the functions will depend on the type of mouse that you have. Find the mouse settings under **Options**. Type Options and then select the user **Preferences** as shown here in A-6. The right click options will come up and you can customize them.

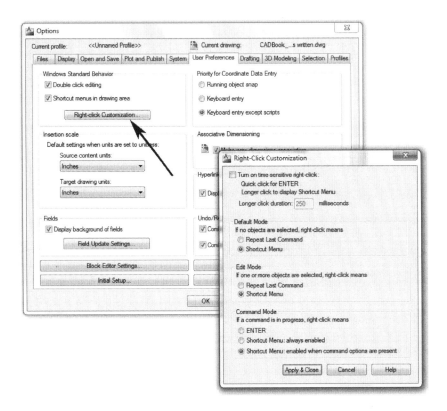

Fig A-6

The size of your grip boxes and your pick boxes can be set under the **Selection** tab.

To set how quickly the mouse wheel zooms in and out type **zoomfactor** and enter a number to determine how fast the mouse wheel zooms in and out. For most operations a setting of 40 to 60 is best.

Enter can be done with a right click of the mouse for many commands. Use the trial and error method to figure out which. That is easier than explaining each variation. As always, use the Undo button if you get into trouble.

There are a variety of right click options and the best way to discover them is to right click at various times during the different functions and see what happens. You can always undo if you get into a weird place.

Mouse Wheel

The mouse wheel is used for moving around in the drawing and zooming in and out. Holding the wheel down allows you to move the drawing (called panning or to pan), turning the wheel zooms in and out.

Nodes and Points

Points and nodes are basically the same thing. You can set the style of the point or node in the **Point Style** settings box. Type ptype to open this box. You can alter **individual points** with the **Properties palette**.

Ortho

Ortho restricts the movement of objects (and the drawing of lines) to 90 degree angles: vertical and horizontal. Use the **F8** button on the keyboard to toggle this on and off, or click on the button at the bottom of the workspace screen.

Object snap

Object snap pinpoints a particular point for attaching lines or other objects. If you type in Osnap, a **Drafting Settings** window will open. Set the points where you want the Osnap to automatically attach objects.

You can turn the Osnap function on and off with the **F3** button on your keyboard. Or use the button at the bottom of the screen (shown in Fig 1-1)

It is important to understand that when you are moving or copying an object that the **base point** you use to grab that object (and osnap it to where you are copying or moving it) can be **anywhere** on the screen. **It does not have to be located on the object itself**. This you will use quite often.

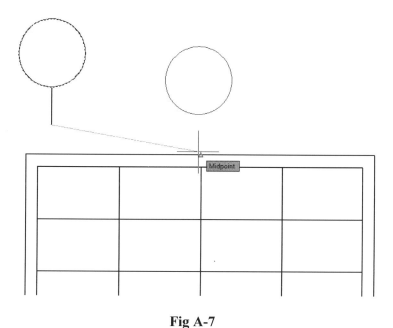

Fig A-7

Fig A-7 demonstrates how this functions. The circle was drawn at the upper left. To copy it we select the circle, but **do not select the line. Enter**. When prompted for a **base point**, click on the **lower end** of the **line**. *This will copy the circle but not the line*. It will snap the circle to the midpoint shown, but it will be copied to a point offset from the midpoint by the distance equal to the length of the line.

It would be the same if you copied the circle and line, then erased the line.

Object snap settings

To set object snaps (called osnaps) **right click** on the **Osnap button** at the bottom of the screen. The osnap settings window will come up. Here you can select the osnap points that you want to snap to.

Page Setup (first time)

First time page set up is detailed in Chapter 1. That is the quick start version, however, and much of the setup is scattered throughout the book. Here is the setup in order of steps.

You must set the **units**. You can type units and select the Architectural selection. Insertion scale should be inches. Angle will be Decimal Degrees. Precision can be set to 0.00 (that is close enough for this type of drawing—of course other types of drafting will require more precision).

In some templates AutoCad asks that you set up Extents. I have always ignored this and cannot find any downside to that. But if you wish you can set the limits of the drawing area (type: limits). If you are drawing something small then this can be the size of your paper (the paper size you will print on). Something large, like a house with many views will require a huge area for drawing. You can change it later. But it should be many times larger than the house. If you do not set the extents, the **program automatically recognizes the extent of what you have drawn** at any particular stage in the drawing process; so when you zoom all the way out it will always show just what you have drawn. The Zoom All button will do this automatically (or type z <e> a <e>).

You will eventually need to set up Text Styles, dimension styles, and layers. But you can start drawing at this point.

Text Styles are set by clicking on the Text Style button on the Annotation palette (click the down arrow next to Annotation) or type **style <e>**. Pick a font (set it as regular for now in the Font Style window); set the height of the text (this can be altered, later, in the Text Editing ribbon that opens when you use the Mtext function). See Chapter 1, 1.21.

If you want to use **Annotative text**, set the height to the size of text that you will want to print out on paper.

If you do not want to use annotative text, you must set the actual size of the text in relation to your drawing. These sizes also can be changed in the Text Editor ribbon that opens each time you use Mtext (it opens when you open a mtext box). Set your style **Current**.

Open a Mtext window (type mt and enter, then click on the screen in two points to open a box) and look through the options available in the Text Editor ribbon.

You can turn on the Text formatting Toolbar by clicking on the arrow next to More in the Options panel of the Text Editor ribbon. Select Editor Settings then Show Toolbar.

Dimension styles are set in the Dimension Styles Manager dialog box. You can access that by clicking on the Dimension Style manager button in the Annotation palette or **type: dimstyle**. You start out with a Standard and an Annotative Style preset. To create a new style: click on one of these two and then the "**New**" button. This is all detailed in Chapter 1 Section 1.23.

Whether you use the Annotative feature or set your text height manually, you will need to know what scale you intend to plot to (or print out). Determine this before you create dimensions or text on your drawing.

Leaders are set with the dimension style, except you must also set the leader settings under the **Leader Settings** (see Leaders in this appendix for details).

Layers are used to create different line styles (dashed for instance) and to create different layers that can be turned on or off. Many architectural drafters use many (sometimes many, many) layers. There are reasons for this, but for simple house plans, eight or ten layers is enough. Use a text layer, a dimension layer, and set up a construction line layer for temporary reference lines that you do not want to be part of the final drawing. Use a Hatch layer for hatch and gradients.

The set up for layers is through the **Layer Properties Manager**. You can see a graphic of this in Chapter 1, Section 1.18. You can alter the properties of any object by using the **Properties** palette—select an object then right click and select Properties to open the palette. This is especially useful for setting the dashed lines to the right scale. It is also very useful for overriding text in the dimensions (Chapter 2, Section 2.11).

This is most of what is involved in the initial setup. But you can just follow along with the book and it will guide you through all of this as it is required.

Panning

Use the center mouse wheel. Press down and hold. You will see a little hand. Use the hand to move around in the drawing. If you don't have a mouse with a center wheel, buy one. If you won't or cannot then your best option is using the different Zoom commands to move around in the workspace. Try out the different settings. **Zoom All** shows everything on the screen. **Zoom Window** zooms in on the area you select. These two work well in combination. The **Zoom Dynamic** is very helpful for this, also.

Plotting

The book walks you through the set up for plotters and printers. This begins in Chapter 3 where most of the details are explained.

An important thing to remember is that you have to **plot to file** if you are not going to print out directly to a printer. So if you are going to take your drawing to a blueprinter and have it printed out (called plotting in the jargon of drafting), then you need to create a file that can be emailed or copied onto a dvd or flashdrive.

Find the setting for that in the **Plotter Setup wizard**, which you open by selecting the **Output** tab and then: **Plotter Manager**. Select: **Add-A-Plotter Wizard**. As you go through the windows in the wizard you will come to the **Add Plotter-Ports** page. At the top you will see a radio button for **Plot to File**. That is what you want. You are plotting on a particular printer but not directly through a wire—rather you are delivering the file to the printer via disc, email or flash drive. Make sure you save the file to some place on your computer where you can find it— the desktop works well while you are working on the project.

Make sure to turn off any layers that you do not want to be plotted or printed. Do this in the **Layer Properties Manager**. Click on the little **printer icon** so that it has a red circle with diagonal line in it.

Dashed lines sometimes show up as solid lines in the viewport (and plot as solid lines on paper). If you don't see your dashed lines in the viewport you can check in the print preview. If they are not there you need to reset your paper space line type scale. Type **psltscale** and set the value to **0**. Then type: **Regenall**. The lines should appear dashed. If not see dashed lines in this appendix.

Points

See Nodes.

Polar Co-ordinates

Polar co-ordinates refer to the degrees of arc from the **starting point** (0) which is set by default as left to right horizontal on the screen. Fig A-8 shows how this works. When you draw lines by using coordinates this is the system that is used for the angles of the lines. This is, also, the system that is used for rotation. As you can see it is counter clockwise in its orientation. You can enter negative numbers to get a clockwise rotation.

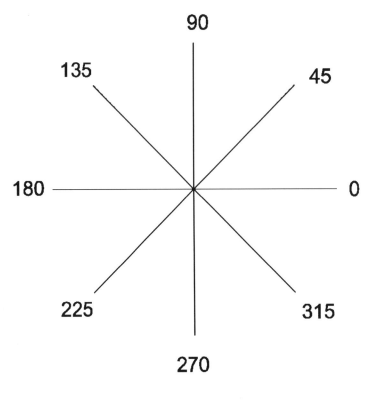

Fig A-8

Polar Tracking

Polar Tracking can be set from the Draft Settings window. You can set the number of degrees that you want it to recognize. This is useful for drawings with a lot of angles and especially for isometric drawings. Try it to see how it works. Right click on the Polar Tracking button at the bottom of the screen (next to osnap) to get at the settings.

If it is not there click on the Customization button on the Status bar (three horizontal lines to the far right in the bottom of the screen). Turn on the status bar buttons you want.

Printer Driver

Many office or home printers require a driver. You must download the driver to the computer that you are using. Many printers come with a disc that contains the driver. If that is not available you may need to go online and search for your driver on the website of the company that manufactures the printer.

Properties palette

Properties is very useful for a plethora of things. You can make adjustments to any object here. This is especially useful for the purpose of overriding text in dimensions, you can change the scale of your dashed lines, you can alter line spacing, and all manner of other adjustments.

To open the Properties palette, select an object, then right click and select Properties from the window that appears. You can also type **properties** or find it on the Properties palette—click on the little arrow in the lower right corner.

Saving
The system saves automatically (newer versions). You can change the time between saves. Type **Options** then the **Open and Save** tab.

Screen shot
Screen shots are copies of what you see on the computer display (screen) at the time you record the screen shot. The method for creating a screen shot is different for each brand of computer. The most common is to hold down the **function key** and press the keyboard button that says **screen shot**. These are often blue or a light colored designation on the keyboard, so look closely.

You may have to consult the user manual for your computer or look online for the method that works with your computer.

To **place** the **screen shot** in the destination drawing use **Ctrl+V**. Hold down the Ctrl button on your keyboard and press V. Then click on the screen where you want to insert the screen shot.

If it is a very small item, relative to the overall drawing, then you must keep track of where you place it or you may have difficulty finding it later.

Selection window
Selection windows cover areas of the drawing for selection (for example to copy) as opposed to clicking on a single object (for example: several lines as opposed to one single line).

There are two types of selection windows. The **green selection window** opens when you click on the screen and move the cursor to the left. The **blue selection window** opens when you click on the screen and move the cursor to the right.

The **green** selection window selects **everything touched by** the green shading (even if it doesn't completely encompass the object).

The **blue** selection window only selects items that are **located completely within** the blue shading.

So, to select a line: it must be completely covered by the blue shading to be selected, but only touched by the green shading to be selected.

There are now (finally) two ways to use the selection windows. One is to click, let go of the mouse button, move the mouse and click again on the opposite corner to create a rectangular selection window. The other method is to click on the screen and hold the left mouse button down to create an irregular selection window. Try it both ways to see how this functions.

Figure A-9 shows a green selection window (the blue window works in the opposite direction):

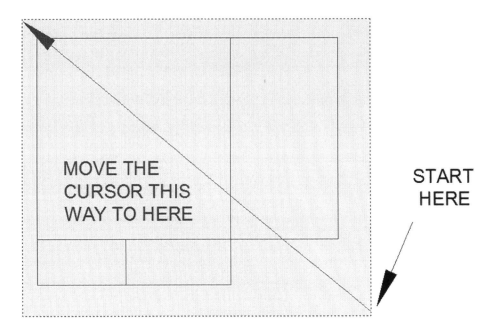

Fig A-9

Fig A-9 shows how to use the green selection window. In this case it completely covers the objects to be copied (the house plan layout), but, in fact, it only needs to touch each element to select it.

The blue selection window works in the opposite direction—start at the left and pull toward the right.

Selection problems
Sometimes a glitch in the system will change the settings so that you cannot select objects. If this happens you should type: **Selectionpreview**, set it to **3**.

Sometimes AutoCAD will not recognize an object in the drawing. This seems to happen most often with text, especially text that has been copied into a drawing. If this happens you may need to move your drawing objects away from the unrecognized object and then you may be able to select and erase the offending unrecognizable objects and replace them. Or you can leave them off to the side of your drawing area. Of course this will mean you must redraw the objects, so this is the last resort when all else fails.

Setup Page
It is a good idea to create a standard page that is already setup with all of your settings for any particular type of drawing (say one for architectural and another for mechanical drawings). See **Page Set Up** in this appendix, then **name** and **save the setup**. Then when you start a new drawing, open this page and save a copy by using the **Save As** selection under **File**. Give it a new name.

Snap From
Snap from is essentially an offset tool. Use it when you want to start a line where there is no Osnap icon (some place other than the end of a line, or intersection of two lines, or a midpoint, etc).

Snap from is demonstrated in Chapter 1, Section 1.11.

Snap from only works if you do **not click** for the **second point** of the **offset**. Read the prompts as you use this command.

Click for the first point, but the second point is entered numerically. Fig A-10 shows how this functions.

Draw a line 20' long. Then click on the **Line** button, hold down the shift key on your key board and right click to open the Osnap menu. Select **From**. **Click** on the **Endpoint** icon as in **A** in **Fig A-10**. Now **hover** over the midpoint icon at **point B—do not click** on it. **Type 7.5'** <e>. The icon at point B must be highlighted when you type 7.5' and <e>. Now move the cursor down until you see the line that starts at point C and click. We are not concerned with the length of this line.

If the icon at B is not visible when you enter the 7.5', the new line (which starts at C) will not be attached to the first line. It may look like it is attached but it will (most likely) be off just a tiny bit. Sometimes you will highlight the icon (as at point B) but, when you let go of the mouse to type, it will shift a bit and the icon will disappear. This will not work. The icon must be visible when you type the offset and enter.

The procedures for Snap From are very precise. If you vary them at all, it will not work.

In spite of this, Snap From is a very useful tool.

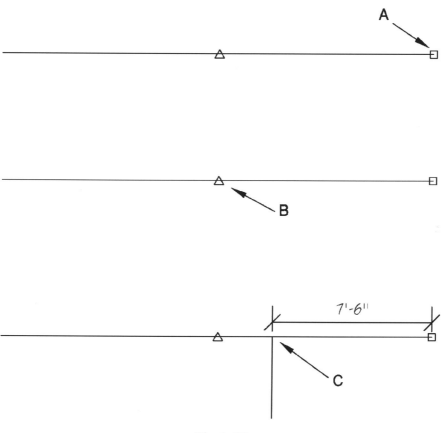

Fig A-10

Spline

Splines are set by pressing the **enter** key on the keyboard **after clicking to set the last point** of the spline. After you set the last point pull the spline line beyond the last point. Pull it way out and move the cursor around to see how it affects the spline. When you see what you want hit the **enter** on your keyboard.

Splines sometimes take a hook at the end when you try to terminate the spline line. You must not move the cursor (as much as that is possible) after you click on the last point of the spline. You can also pull the line way out into space (but no click) before you **enter** to prevent this hook thing from happening.

Start up instructions

See Page Setup for start-up instructions. Or simply start with the introduction and follow the text as all the setup is contained in the lessons.

Stretch

Stretch is one of the most difficult commands to use. It involves understanding what AutoCAD sees as an object. A good way to understand this is to stretch the bathtub that we imported in Chapter 1. Make a copy of the tub. Now click on the **Stretch** button on the **Modify palette**. It will prompt you to select objects. Make a green selection window around the right half of the tub, enter, click on the right side of the tub, and then try to stretch it to the right. Nothing happens. This is because AutoCAD sees the tub as one object.

Now use the **Explode**. Type: explode and enclose the entire tub in a selection window and enter.

Now try the Stretch command again. Create a **green selection window** around the **right half** of the **tub, enter, click** on the **right side** of the tube and **pull** the cursor out to the **right. Click.**

With the explode function you have broken the tub into a series of lines and curves. Now AutoCAD sees these separately and can distinguish which are to be stretched. You have to select only half (or a section of) the object to be stretched. Otherwise the system doesn't know which lines to stretch and which to leave unaltered.

Try this again with a blue selection window—it won't work. This is because the blue selection window only selects objects that are completely covered with the blue shading. Stretch must be used with the green selection window and the green shading can only cover half (or a portion) of the object.

Tables

Tables are explained in Chapter 12 in my book **AutoCAD in 20 Hours**.

I had a glitch with tables where it would not set the correct cell size. I shut down AutoCAD and restarted it and it worked properly.

Text

Text Styles are set by clicking on the **Text Style** button on the **Annotation palette** or type **style** (enter). The setup is explained in **Chapter 1 Section 1.21**. Pick a font (set it as regular for now in the Font Style window); set the height of the text (this can be altered in the Text Formatting bar that opens when you use the Mtext function).

If you set up the **Text Formatting Toolbar** (Fig A-11) to open it will open when you use Mtext. To turn on the text formatting tool bar type **mtexttoolbar** and set the variable to **1**. Or set it on the **Text Editor** ribbon that opens when you open a Mtext window. Find it on the **Options** palette under **More/Editor Settings/Show Toolbar**.

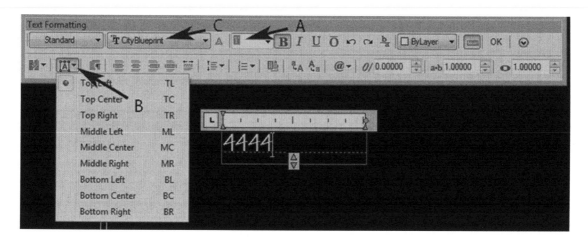

Fig A-11

Sometimes the **text box** and **ruler** are **huge** and run off the screen out into infinity. If this happens type: **mtextcolumn** and set the value to 0. If it still persists with the huge box then type **mtextfixed** and set the value to 0. If it still persists then open a mtext box and in the Options palette (Text Editor ribbon) click on More, then Editor Settings, then turn on the Always display as WYSIWYG. This means: what you see is what you get (no I am not joking).

If the **Text Formatting** bar is in the way, **move it** with the blue strip at the top: position the cursor on the blue bar and hold down the left mouse button to grab it and move it.

Set the **height** of the text in the window **A** in **Fig A-11**. Set the **style** at **C**. The **justification** can be set at **B**. You can also set this on the Text Editor ribbon.

If you are going to edit text that is already there, you must highlight the text first. Click at the beginning or the end of the section of text you wish to edit and run the cursor over the text while you hold down the left mouse button, then to shade it. Then make the changes you desire.

HUGE TEXT Problem: If you are getting **huge text,** when you do not want to get huge text, then the problem may be that the Annotation Scale in the window at the bottom right of your screen is set to some scale. You want it to read 1:1 with non-annotative text styles. Set it thusly and that should fix the problem.

If you want to use **Annotative** text, set the height to the size of text that you will want to print out on paper (1/8" for example).

If you do not want to use annotative text then you must set the actual size of the text in relation to your drawing. This subject is covered in detail in **AutoCAD in 20 Hours**, Chapter 13. These sizes can be changed in the Text Formatting bar (Fig A-11) that opens each time you use Mtext or on the Text Editor ribbon that also opens with the Mtext window.

When you set a new text style set that style **Current** in the **Text Style** window.

Everything about text cannot be explained here. Most of it is simply typing like any word processing program. The only thing that is difficult is the size (or scale) of the text. See Chapter 1 Section 1.21.

Trim and Extend

Trim and Extend can be a bit difficult at times. They don't always function properly. As with a lot of commands at certain times (especially it seems when files get real large—as they tend to do with architectural plans) the buttons don't respond very well. In this case it helps to **double click**. That usually get the message through.

Trim and Extend both work pretty much the same. You can use them two ways. The method that is the most useful is to click on the button then **immediately** hit the **enter** key on your keyboard. This creates a cutting tool for trim that trims everything you click on back to any line that crosses it. For Extend it extends everything you click on to the next crossing line or object.

But extend doesn't always work this way because it may not recognize which side of the line you are extending and it might not recognize the crossing line that you want to extend to.

Extend won't work unless there is a line (or object) in the crossing plane of the line to be extended. It must run into another line or object.

And trim won't work if there is not another line or object crossing the line you are trimming.

This can be difficult to determine because AutoCAD works to extremely fine tolerances and it can appear that two lines are touching when they are not. So if trim is not working, zoom way in to see if the lines are crossing.

The other way to use trim and extend is to click on the button and then follow the prompts (do not enter immediately). Trim will ask you to select objects. This is the reverse of what many might think, it is asking for the trim line, not the line to be trimmed. Then you enter and click on the line to be trimmed.

The same for extend. When you click on the Extend button, and do not enter right away, it will prompt you to select objects. This is the line to which you want to extend to. Then enter and click on the line you want to extend.

If you forget just try it both ways and you will rediscover what the prompts are referring to.

Typing Commands

All of the commands can be typed instead of using the buttons. But if you do this you must **type** the **command** and then **enter**. These two steps are the same as clicking on the button. Or to put it another way, clicking a button equals typing the command and then pressing the enter key on the keyboard.

This can lead to a bit of confusion because the commands in this book are just clicking on the button. As an example, the Trim (and Extend) functions two different ways. One way involves clicking on the button and then hitting the enter key immediately. This creates a trimming tool. But if you **type** Trim you must **enter twice** immediately to get the trim to function this way—once to set the Trim command, and once to set the trimming tool function.

The buttons equal the **typed command *and* enter**. So if the procedure calls for clicking a button and entering, to type that same command you must type the command, enter, and enter again. This is difficult to explain but easy to see if you try it. The button sets the command in motion. A typed command just sits on the command line until you press enter to set the command in motion. Try this a few times to see how this works.

UCS

The UCS is a point of orientation on the work space. In two dimension drawing it has two axes—X and Y. This can be used to set points in the workspace; it can also be used to draw lines or place objects based on co-ordinate input. In other words you can type in a pair of co-ordinates for the starting point of a line and another pair for the end point. This is not very efficient for most objects, but it is an excellent way to place points in an open field (as we do with the plot plan in **AutoCAD in 20 Hours**, Chapter 4).

The origin of the UCS is the point from which everything is measured. It can be set anywhere in the workspace or it can be left in the lower left corner of the drawing area (this is called World UCS). Either way it works basically the same. To set a point (or node) click on the **Point** button (on the Draw palette) or type po and read the prompts. It asks for co-ordinates and these can be entered as a distance from the origin point of the UCS—horizontal first, then a comma, then vertical.

Lines are the same: type two co-ordinates for the start of the line and two for the end.

The **settings** for UCS are on the **Coordinates** panel on the View ribbon. Turn it on or off with the UCS button to the far left of the View ribbon.

Set it to a particular point on your drawing by clicking on the **Origin** button in the middle of the coordinates panel on the View ribbon and then click on the point in your drawing where you want to set an origin point. Now you can use this to enter co-ordinates for many different objects.

Viewports

Viewports can be locked so they do not accidentally get altered. In the Layout tab that you are using set the Model/Paper button to Paper. Now run the cursor over the line that represents the edge of the viewport, it will highlight—click on it when it is highlighted to select it. Do not confuse the margin line for the viewport line. When the viewport line is selected (the blue grip boxes will appear) right click. There you will see the setting for locking the viewport. Remember that it is locked if you need to change things later.

The lines of the paper space can change, sometimes spontaneously (a glitch). The settings to get it back are in the Options dialog box. Type options and click on the Display tab and then the box next to Display paper background.

Chapter 3 covers the basics of viewports. Viewports are covered in great detail in AutoCAD in 20 Hours.

Units

Set the units by typing **units** or access it from the **Format tab** at the top of the page. Often AutoCAD **does not set the units correctly in the Startup box.** So if you have problems set it here, it should stick.

Zoom

There are a number of zoom options in AutoCad. They are as follows:

Mouse wheel set the zoomfactor (how fast it zooms in and out) by typing **zoomfactor** and enter a number.
Zoom Window—the area enclosed in the selection window (that you create) fills the screen.
Zoom Dynamic—zooms out and then creates a box that can be adjusted in size and then enter to zoom in. This is essentially like using Zoom All and Zoom Window together in one command.
Zoom Scale—uses some complicated formula.
Zoom Center—pinpoint a spot on the workspace and enter a number that represents the size of the zoom area.
Zoom Object—zooms in on selected object.
Zoom in—zooms into the current screen.
Zoom out—zooms out in the current screen.
Zoom All—zooms out to show the entire workspace in use.
Zoom Extents—zooms out to show the entire area covered in the extents that have (maybe) been set (how is this different from Zoom All?)

Type **z** <e> and then the **first letter** of the **zoom command** type as in **A** for Zoom **All** (**z** <e> then **a** <e>) or **W** for Zoom **Window** (**z** <e> then **w** <e>). There are also buttons in the lower right corner of the Navigate panel on the View ribbon, but it is easier just to type these commands.

Appendix I

Appendix II—Location of Buttons and Settings

Most of the buttons and command paths can be found in the Help menu. Click on Help at the top of the screen or press the F1 key. Scroll down and select Commands. An alphabetical list will come up and then follow the links to the command you are trying to find.

Many of the command buttons are co-located with other command buttons. The Rectangle command button is co-located with the Polygon button; the Linear dimension command button is co-located with other dimension command buttons. So when you are looking for a button on a particular palette, and do not see it, click on the down arrow next to the visible buttons to see what appears.

Remember that all commands and settings can be done by typing in the command line. The typed command can be found in the Command Reference as referenced above. The most common are often the first letter of the command, sometimes the first two or three letters will do, but you can usually type the whole word.

A number of commands are available upon right clicking the mouse. Right click on the open screen and see what comes up. At the bottom you will see Options. This is a quick way to get at the options should you need to switch back and forth a bit. Try right clicking at different points in any given command process to see what is available.

Also the most recently used commands can be accessed from the menu that you get from a right click when no command is in process.

You can add or remove ribbon tabs and palettes by right clicking anywhere on the ribbon. There you will find the Show Tabs selection menu and the Show Panels menu (Panels and Palettes are the same).

<u>AutoCad Appendix IV—Plan Set</u>

This appendix is the complete set of plans for this house and a few close-up details.

If you want to learn to draw a full set of plans visit the AutoCAD in 20 Hours website: Autocadin20hours.com

Of course it is difficult to get good detail on this size (8.5 x 11) paper when the subject is meant to be displayed on paper that is 36 x 24 inches. A house is a large object to draw. For an expandable view go to the website. There you will find a **full set of plans available in PDF format**. These can be zoomed and all the detail is very clear in that format.

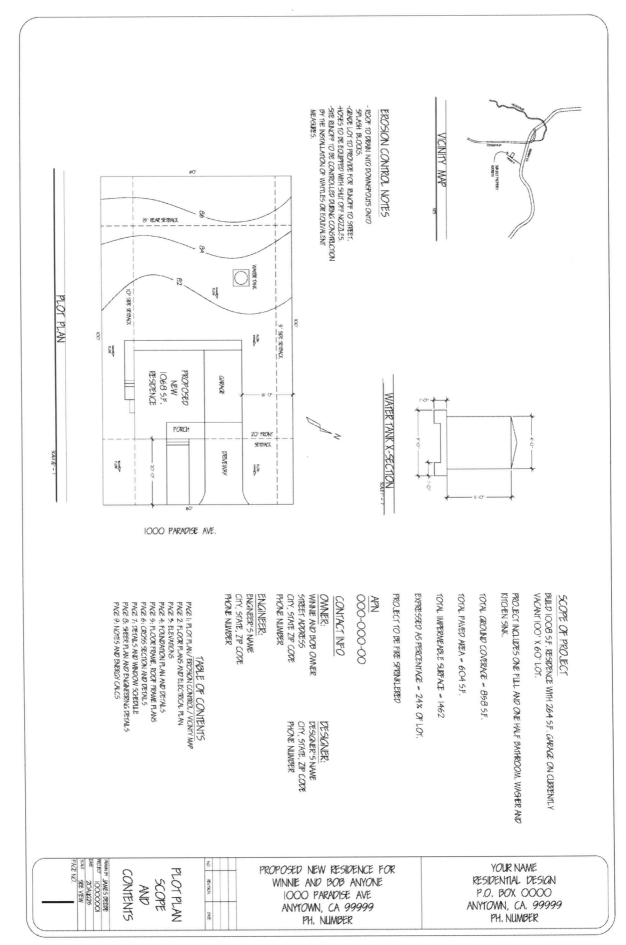

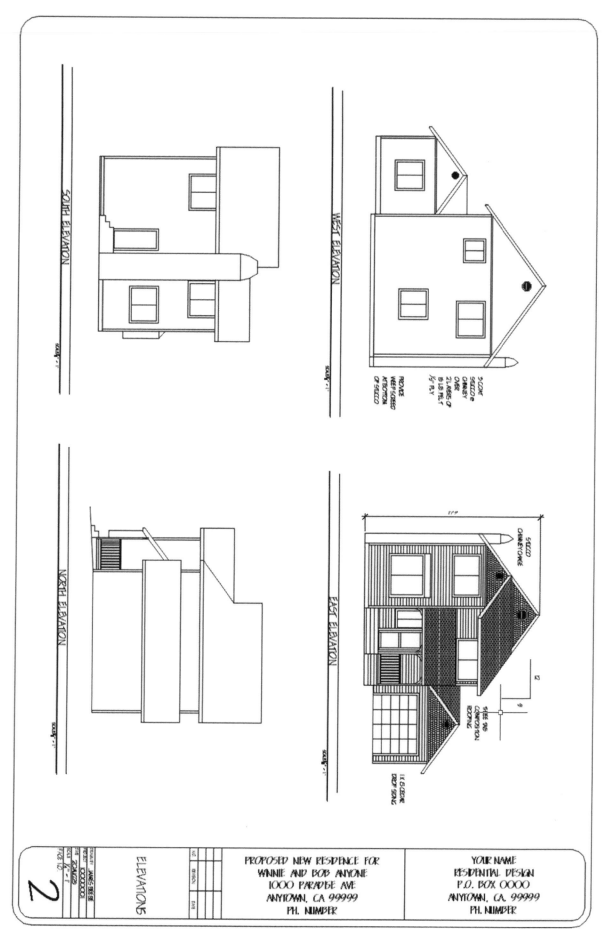

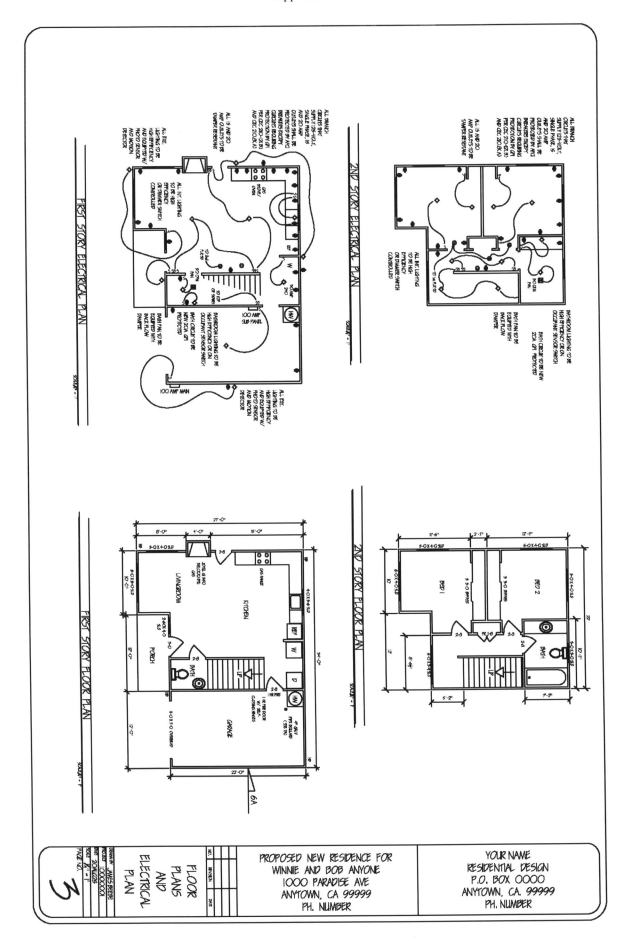

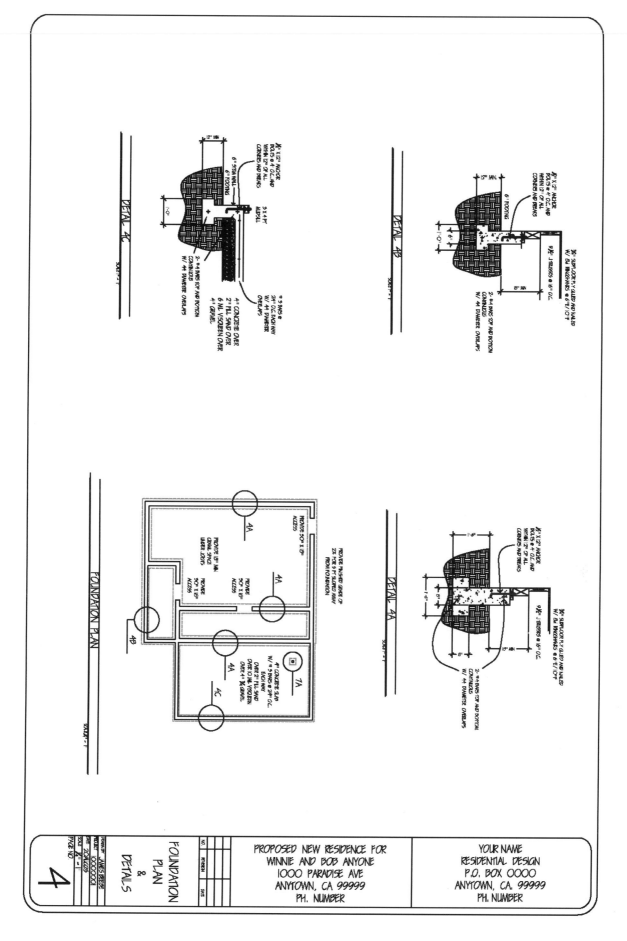

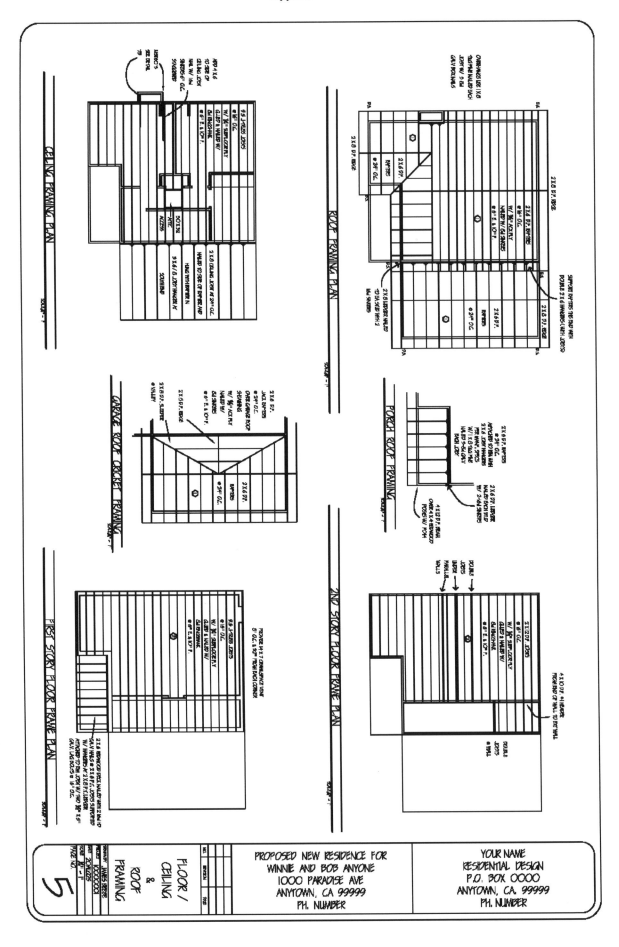

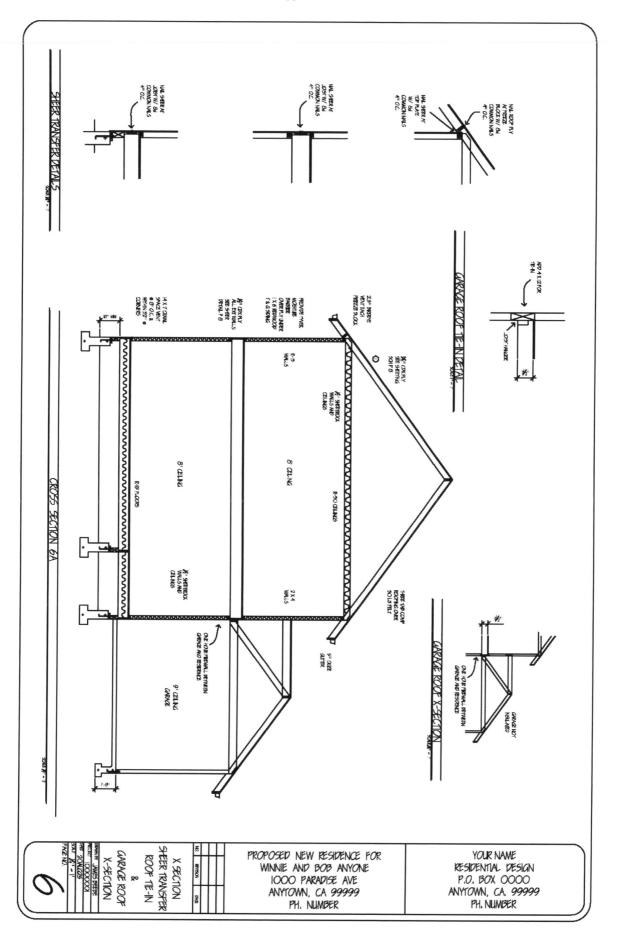

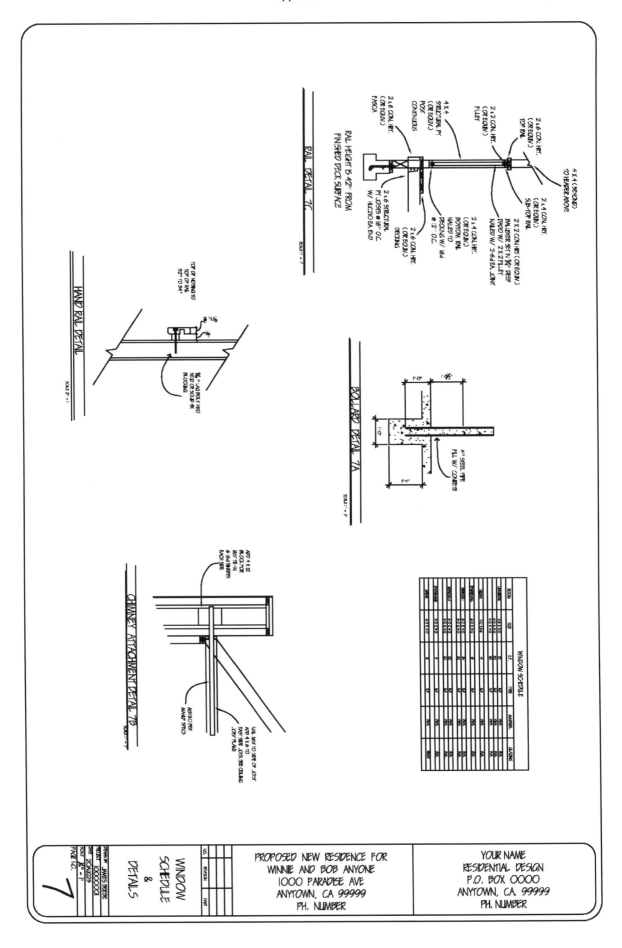

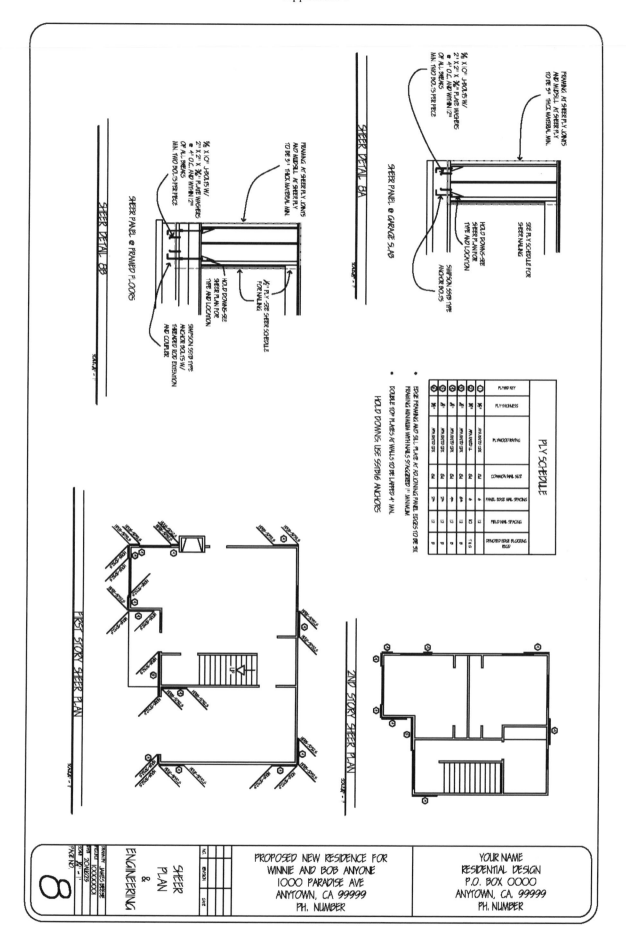

GENERAL CONSTRUCTION NOTES

1- CURRENT APPLICABLE CODES 2010 CBC, 2010 MECH, PLUMB & ELECT CODES
2- PLUMBING FIXTURES SHALL COMPLY WITH THE FOLLOWING STANDARDS
 -TOILETS TO BE HIGH EFFICIENCY - 1.6 GALS / FLUSH MAX.
 -SHOWER HEAD - 2.5 GALS / MIN MAX.
 -LAVATORY FAUCET - 2.2 GALS / MIN MAX.
3- ALL DOORS AND WINDOWS TO BE CAULKED FOR SEAL TO WEATHER STRIPPED.
4- ALL EXT DOORS TO BE WEATHER STRIPPED.
5- CAULK ALL VENTS AND PIPES AT PENETRATION OF EXT. MEMBRANE.
6- PROVIDE TYVEK TYPE MOISTURE BARRIER AT EXT. WALLS UNDER SIDING.
7- ALL EXT HANDRAILS TO BE OF CORROSION RESISTANCE EX. GALV, ANODIZED,
 STAINLESS OR ALUMINUM.
8- ALL CONSTRUCTION LUMBER TO BE #2 & BTR DF UNLESS SPECIFIED.
9- ALL WOOD EXPOSED TO THE WEATHER TO BE PT OR APPROVED NATURALLY
 DECAY RESISTANT SPECIES.
 -PROVIDE 1" SEPARATION BETWEEN NON-DECAY RESISTANT WOOD AND EARTH.
10- ALL FASTENERS INTO PT LUMBER TO BE HOT DIPPED ZINC COATED GALVANIZED,
 ANODIZED, OR STAINLESS STEEL.
11- ALL MEASUREMENTS TO BE FIELD VERIFIED.
12- PROVIDE 12" X 12" REMOVABLE ACCESS PANEL FOR ALL PLUMBING FIXTURES W/
 CONCEALED SLIP JOINT CONNECTORS.
13- SHOWER ENCLOSURE TO BE TEMPERED GLASS.
14- PROVIDE NON-REMOVABLE BACK FLOW DEVICES AT ALL HOSE BIBS.
15- PROVIDE WEEP SCREED AT BOTTOM OF ALL STUCCO SECTIONS.

YOUR NAME RESIDENTIAL DESIGN P.O. BOX 0000 ANYTOWN, CA. 99999 PH. NUMBER	PROPOSED NEW RESIDENCE FOR WINNIE AND BOB ANYONE 1000 PARADISE AVE ANYTOWN, CA 99999 PH. NUMBER	NOTES	6

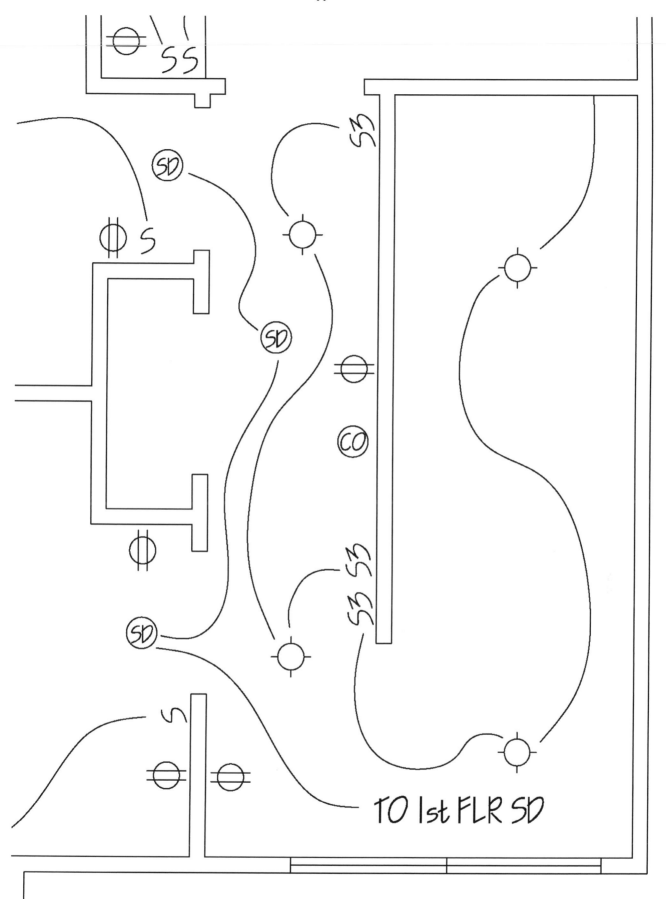

TO 1st FLR SD

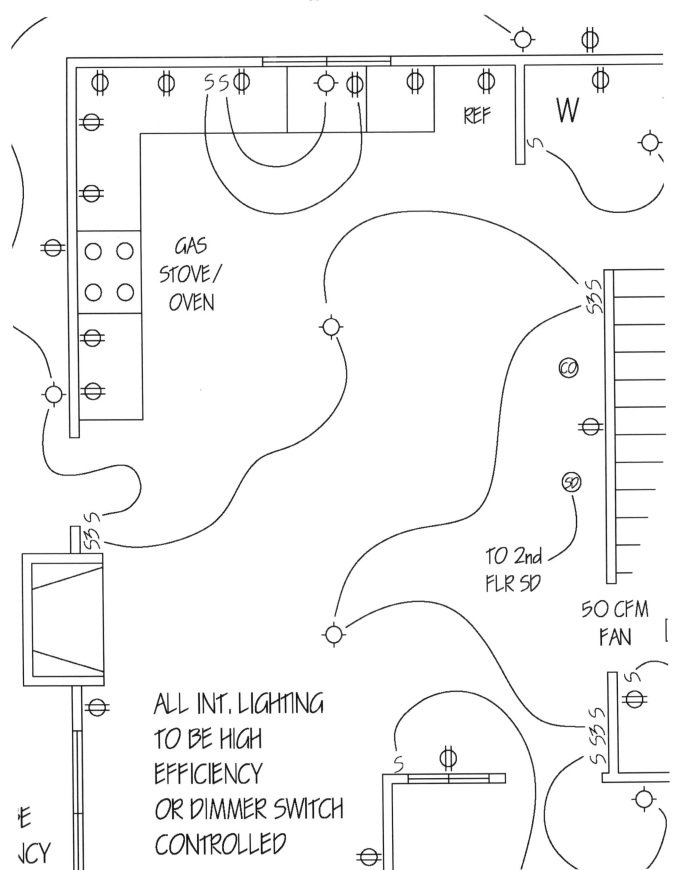

SS

REF

W

GAS
STOVE/
OVEN

CO

SD

TO 2nd
FLR SD

50 CFM
FAN

ALL INT. LIGHTING
TO BE HIGH
EFFICIENCY
OR DIMMER SWITCH
CONTROLLED

E
JCY

S

Detail of Chimney Tie-in from Page 7

Index

Printed in Great Britain
by Amazon

67322622R00086